You Don't Know Dick!

✦

An Onomastic Reference Compendium

You Don't Know Dick!

✦

An Onomastic Reference Compendium

Larry Rogak

iUniverse, Inc.
New York Lincoln Shanghai

You Don't Know Dick!
An Onomastic Reference Compendium

iUniverse books may be ordered through booksellers or by contacting:

iUniverse
2021 Pine Lake Road, Suite 100
Lincoln, NE 68512
www.iuniverse.com
1-800-Authors (1-800-288-4677)

ISBN-13: 978-0-595-35433-7 (pbk)
ISBN-13: 978-0-595-79929-9 (ebk)
ISBN-10: 0-595-35433-5 (pbk)
ISBN-10: 0-595-79929-9 (ebk)

Printed in the United States of America

To my son Brendan, who walks in my footsteps
yet leaves his own unique set of tracks.

"Without music to decorate it, time is just a bunch of boring production deadlines or dates by which bills must be paid."

—Frank Zappa

Contents

Introduction

In one sense, this book is really stupid, and maybe you should feel a little guilty about reading it. But perhaps that's far too elitist a position. After all, this book is far less stupid than any "reality TV" show, and look how many people sit like drugged Rhesus monkeys in front of their monitors every night, gazing bleary-eyed, watching boring, ordinary people interact in stupid, contrived situations.

This book is also far less stupid than many songs, particularly rap and hip hop. If entertainers can make millions of dollars singing about bitches and ho's, or about how other singers are punks and cowards, then certainly a book like this one falls into a higher slot on the stupidity spectrum than they do.

And this book is also less stupid than many of the books which become best-sellers, especially when they are written by people who have little or nothing to say but who have had their 15 minutes of fame. Like Paris Hilton. *Confessions of An Heiress*?? Give me a break. What can she confess to that we haven't already seen her do on the internet? Same goes for any autobiography by, or a biography of, anybody under 30. And it seems that every time some unknown person gets involved in a highly-publicized incident, a book comes out. The incident lasted four minutes and yet they write a book about it that takes 2 hours to read.

So maybe this book isn't so stupid after all. It's brilliant compared to a lot of the crap out there.

Comedy is a complex subject. There are many different elements that can make a joke, or a presentation, funny. One of the elements of comedy is the "double meaning," and its nearly-identical cousin, the pun. Here's a really bad joke using a double-meaning word, just for illustration purposes:

Man: "I just bought a new air conditioner."
Woman: "That's cool."

Ok, not the funniest joke in the world—unless it's the first time you've heard it. But what makes it a joke at all is that the word "cool" has a double meaning: "low temperature" and "good."

Try the same joke, without a double meaning word:

Man: "I just bought a new air conditioner."
Woman: "Fuck off."

See, that's funny, too. But for a different reason. First of all, "fuck" is always a shocker word. You can stick it almost anyplace and get a laugh. But the reason it's funny here (and almost anywhere else) is the sudden reversal of direction. You didn't see the joke going in that direction. That makes it funny. If the woman's response was, "That's nice," it wouldn't be funny.

A pun is a play on words. Here's a pun joke:

A woman has twins and gives them up for adoption. One of them goes to a family in Egypt and is named "Ahmal." The other goes to a family in Spain, they name him "Juan." Years later, Juan sends a picture of himself to his birth mother. Upon receiving the picture, she tells her husband that she wishes she also had a picture of Ahmal. Her husband responds, "They're twins. If you've seen Juan, you've seen Ahmal."

Didja like that? You want another one, don't you? Why don't you just buy a book of puns then, stupid? Ok, you're here already, you're sitting, you're reading. I'll give you a couple more.

Two Eskimos sitting in a kayak were chilly, but when they lit a fire in the craft, it burned a hole in the bottom and it sank. Proving once again: that you can't have your kayak and heat it, too.

Stop those groans. You like it. You want more.

In ancient Rome, deli workers were told that they could eat anything they wanted during the lunch hour. Anything that is, except the smoked salmon. Thus were created the world's first anti-lox breaks.

Enough puns. Back to the subject.

Here's another type of joke:

A woman walks up to a man in a bar, sticks her tongue in his ear and whispers, "I'll do anything you want for $500." The man says, "Great! Paint my house."

See? That's funny because you didn't see it coming. The unexpected twist is another element of comedy.

What does any of this have to do with dicks, you're asking? Have a little patience, willya?

As recently as the 1970s, you couldn't talk about dicks in public. It was considered too vulgar. Fortunately, our society has become more open in general, or more vulgar, depending on your point of view.

Former President Clinton, bless his surgically-repaired heart, did so much to bring the dick out of the closet and into our living rooms. Thanks to the Monica Lewinsky scandal, the American public got to hear all about his dick, where he takes it out, who he waves it at, where he sticks it, which way it bends, and everything else you might want to know about it, and it was all brought to us in our living rooms courtesy of Ken Starr and the American news media, which dutifully reported all these details as "news."

And of course, once the dick was out of the bag, so to speak, it could never be shoved back in. The word "penis," once a word which could never be uttered on television, is now a standard part of every sitcom script.

Of course, television can't yet *show* a penis. This body part, which 50% of the American public can see merely by dropping their trousers, and which 49.9% of the rest of the public can see merely by asking (and to a large degree, even without asking), somehow becomes an outrage if it were to be shown in public. So for now we can talk about it, but we can't see it. But just give it time. The dick will force its way into our living rooms eventually.

Everyone knows that "Dick" has been the "official" nickname for Richard for centuries (see **The Origin of Dick**, below). And for over 100 years, "dick" has been a popular slang word for "penis." So right away, we have the double meaning, which is one of the Pillars of Humor.

But we have even more than that with "dick." We have a word which *is strictly prohibited in polite company*, but which is also a common name for a man. So you can't say "I'm really proud of my dick" to a group of your mother's friends (unless perhaps you're a child in the Osbourne family), but you could say to them "I'm really proud of Dick," if your brother Dick just graduated from medical school.

Shocking obscenity and common name—such is the dual nature of Dick.

Everyone has heard of dick jokes. Just to refresh your recollection, here are a few classics, plus some I wrote myself:

My dick is so big, it has a doorman and a lobby.

My dick is so big, it has a horizon.

My dick is so big, it doesn't return Spielberg's calls.

My dick is so big, other guys' dicks call it Mr. Dick.

My dick is so big, it still has snow on top in summertime.

My dick is so big, it has investors.

My dick is so big, it's going condo.

My dick is so big, by law I have to hang a red flag on the end of it when I'm driving.

My dick is so big, I can smuggle Mexicans into the country in it.

My dick is so big, people aspire to climb it.

My dick is so big, it sits in for Letterman.

My dick is so big, I had to get a zoning variance for it.

My dick is so big, my cell phone gets reception everywhere.

My dick is so big, it shows up on satellite photos.

My dick is so big, it has an opening act.

My dick is so big, Starbucks now sells coffee in Tall, Vente, Grande and My Dick.

My dick is so big, it has cable.

My dick is so big, it's not allowed on parkways.

My dick is so big, it gets comped in Las Vegas.

My dick is so big, one of Albert Einstein's theories predicted it.

My dick is so big, *it* jerks *me* off.

My dick is so big, it has gravity. Several smaller dicks orbit it.

What I have done in this book, is to create an entire new genre of dick joke: Dick Names. Well, I didn't exactly *create* it as much as *discover* it and *identify* it and make it available to the public. You know: like Marie Curie did with radium. Like Pamela Anderson did with silicone.

The name Dick by itself is not much of a joke. Okay, we know it has a double meaning. But how many times can you laugh at it? Not much, after you're 8 years old. Unless you're a *real* retard.

But combine "Dick" with a surname that happens to be a word that "works" with Dick, and you have a joke. Imagine you go to work tomorrow and you're called into a meeting. At the meeting a man you've never seen before, a funny looking bald guy, stands up and announces,

> *"As of today I'm your new supervisor. My name is Dick Head. I prefer to be called Mr. Head, but perhaps after we get to know each other you can call me Dick. Actually, my son is Dick Head Junior. So around my house, I'm known as Big Dick and my son is Little Dick. But since my son doesn't work here, there's no need for you to call me Big Dick. I'm just plain old Dick to you."*

Now, by this time, your coffee has come out of your nose about three times already and your napkins are too saturated to use any more. Half the guys in the room can't stand up because they have piss stains on their pants like a kid in kindergarten.

When somebody is named Dick Head, that's a dick joke.

"Why, that's the most immature thing I've ever heard of," says some candy-ass. "It's not these people's faults what their name is," the candy-ass continues.

Let me answer these critics even before this book is published. First of all, we, as Americans, have a constitutional right to laugh at anything, and anyone, we think is funny. If a blind lesbian walks into a fish market and says "hello, girls," we can laugh if we want to without feeling any moral compunctions, because we didn't create the situation; we merely enjoy our *natural* reaction to it.

Secondly—and I think this is very important—nobody forces people named Richard to list themselves in public records and phone books as Dick. If somebody's name is Richard Sucker, or Richard Bigg, then perhaps when they call their local phone company to set up service they should do so under the name Richard, and not Dick, so they don't get listed as Dick Sucker or Dick Bigg. But if they do choose to be listed as Dick, for men, women and children of all ages to see in the G-rated public phone book, then we, as Americans, have the right to laugh at it. And that's what fills the pages of this book.

These Are All Real Names

On almost every page of this book, you will see names that will prompt you to exclaim, "That can't be a real name." I personally guarantee you, the reader, that every single name in this book has been found, by me, during my research, in public phone directories and internet databases.

The Dicks are presented in alphabetical order, in case you couldn't figure that out.

Where the person's name is listed in public phone books, I give the name of the city where they are listed. Not to enable assholes to contact them, but merely for authentication purposes. Where the person has an unlisted number, I give the State in which the person resides, according to the database for unlisted numbers.

We are assuming, for purposes of this book, that anyone named Richard may be called Dick. However, to keep this book's value as genuine reference material as high as possible, I have indicated in each listing whether the name is found as Dick or Richard. Unless I state specifically in a listing that it is found only as Richard, then you may safely assume the official listing is under the name Dick. And if this book indicates that the listing is under the name Dick, then you can safely assume that more exist out there under the name Richard.

"How would you like somebody laughing at your name, asshole?"

That's the question I anticipate coming from some people. Maybe you're even asking it right now. Well, I'll tell you what: I spent my entire childhood having my name ridiculed. Maybe you wouldn't think that my surname, "Rogak," lends itself to teasing by other kids. Well, the world is different when you're a kid, and especially back in the 1960s when kids were less hip than they are today. Many kids, by nature, are mean little fucks. A lot of them get it from their parents. And I grew up in a lower middle class neighborhood where the kids were particularly nasty, coarse and cruel.

We didn't have many "funny" names in my neighborhood. Everyone was either Jewish or Italian or Irish. So you had your Goldbergs and your Cohens and your Gambinis and your Romanos and your Kellys and your Monahans. "Rogak" was, in that assortment of mixed nuts, a yogurt-covered pretzel. I automatically had to spell it as soon as I said it, because nobody seemed to have an idea how to write it. And I got called all kinds of stupid names by the other kids, all variations on whatever ugly rhyme they could come up with for "Rogak."

No, I won't document here exactly what they said. If you're the type of asshole who makes fun of people's names, or did so when you were a kid, figure it out for yourself.

If there hadn't been another kid on the block named **Fink** to divert some of the sadism, my childhood would have been much worse.

So even as I list the names in this book, and laugh, I also empathize. See? I'm a victim too. Now kiss my ass. I also anticipate this next question:

2

"Why would you write a book all about dicks? Wadda you, a homo?"

See, I knew that at least one shithead would ask that. So I carefully prepared my response: "Go fuck yourself." Does that answer your question?

The Origin of Dick

The name Richard is very old, although its origin is disputed. Old English had Richeard, from Ric (ruler) and heard (hard); French had Richart, and Old German had Ricohard. The name Richer was also fairly common until the 13th Century or thereabouts.

In those days, manuscripts, letters, grocery lists, and everything else was written by hand; it was therefore common and easier to use agreed-upon abbreviations. "Rich." was used for "Richer" and "Ric." for "Richard" or "Ricard." Richard and Ricard were equally popular in the Middle Ages, and the abbreviations led naturally to diminutives—such as Rich, Richie, Rick, and Ricket.

Rhyming nicknames were also fairly common in the 12th and 13th centuries, and so we also have Hitch from Rich, Hick and Dick from Rick, and Hicket from Ricket. Some of these later became surnames or parts of surnames. We note that while Dick endures as a nickname, "Hick" has thankfully become obsolete, except when tied to "Dick" in rhymes such as "Hickory, Dickory, Dock."

In the 13th and 14th centuries, "Hick" evolved, however improbably, into "Hudde," from which derives surnames such as "Hudson." W. Bardsley's masterful work, *Dictionary of English and Welsh Surnames* (1901) cites a Latin manuscript that mentions "Ricardus dictus Hudde de Walkden."

Dick and Hick were among the earliest of the rhyming nicknames, first appearing in writing around 1220. Other rhyming nicknames include Polly from Molly, Bob from Rob (from Robert), Bill from Will (from William); and Hodge from Roger. The name Dick (like the name Jack) was used colloquially to mean a man or everyman. The expression "every Tom, Dick, or Harry" attests to the this as a long-established usage; Shakespeare uses "every Tom, Dick, or Francis" in *Henry IV Part I*.

From the usage of Dick to mean average person, other usages appeared. Many other usages. The *Oxford English Dictionary* cites a dick as meaning a type of hard cheese in 1847, which lead to the usage of "spotted dick" (an Irish soda bread with currants and raisins in it; in England, it is made with bread dough rolled up with sugar and raisins inside).

The term "dick" was also used to mean a riding whip, an apron, the mound around a ditch, and an abbreviation for "dictionary" around 1860. Dick also meant a declaration, in which sense the *OED* cites someone writing in 1878 that "I'd take my dying dick" to mean "I'd swear a dying declaration."

The term "dick" came to mean policeman around 1908, and then detective. *The Bank Dick* was a 1940 movie starring W. C. Fields.

The use of "dick" as coarse slang for penis first arises around 1890. Tracking the history of uncouth words is not easy, since such expressions were not generally written down. How "dick" came to be associated with penis is not known, although the riding whip may have pointed the way. So there you have it.

It would be interesting to know who first uttered the immortal words, "Suck my dick." Certainly, if we knew who he was, a sculpture in his honor belongs somewhere.

The foregoing history was adapted (i.e., stolen and given a new paint job) from the website www.StraightDope.com. The Straight Dope is a terrific website which provides readers with accurate answers (i.e., the straight dope) to all those oddball factual questions that nobody seems able to answer. I hope that by saying these nice things about the site, the owners won't sue me for appropriating (that's another word for stealing) their material about the origin of the word "dick."—L.N.R.

Don't Be a Dick

All that being said about what's funny and your right to laugh, let's remember that with rights also go responsibilities.

Some of the people who read this book might be idiots who do not have sufficient respect for the rights of others. So let me put the following *warnings, advisories and disclaimers* here in BIG LETTERS:

WARNING

Do not, under any circumstances, make any attempt to call, write, email, or contact in any manner, directly or indirectly, any of the persons cited in this book. These are real people, ordinary people, who have not done anything to anybody and do not deserve to be harassed, annoyed, or bothered in any way. Especially by idiots.

This book is intended solely for entertainment purposes. It is one thing to laugh privately at somebody's name. It is quite another thing to harass, annoy and intimidate real people.

Crank phone calls, and annoying or harassing communications of any kind, violate any number of local, State and Federal laws, and could lead to arrest and prosecution. As well they should.

There is nothing funny about crank communications. They invade people's privacy and cause consternation and anxiety. I don't care what you saw on *Crank Yankers*; using the telephone or the mails solely to bother people is *against the law,* and it does not make you a comedian, it makes you an asshole. And it could make you a convicted asshole. So *don't do it.*

Cross-References and a Very Brief Lesson in Latin

Many of the names in this book are cross-referenced if they relate to each other in a humorous way. Under each listing, cross-referenced names are indicated by showing the name in **Bold Type** and either preceded by the words "*See,* also," or followed by this notation: (q.v.). The "q.v." is a standard indexing notation which is an abbreviation of the Latin words *quod vide,* which means "which [you should] see [for further information]."

See? You're learning history and Latin in this book. Screw the candy-asses.

And with that, we're almost ready to go into dick land, or, more appropriately, **Dick Land** (q.v.).

Just One Final Note Before You Start…

If you, or a friend, or a loved one, or a co-worker, or the guy you're banging happens to have one of these names, here are a few words of advice before you call your lawyer or go to get the key for the gun cabinet: **RELAX**. Your name is in the phone book of your town, because you put it there. And if your phone number is unlisted, well, it's still unlisted: I didn't give it away. Your name is in the records of Motor Vehicle Bureaus, voter registration records, phone and electric company records, school records, criminal records, and all sorts of other lists which are available, for varying fees, over the internet. All I've done in this book is make the reader aware that your name exists. Everybody you know already knows what your name is. If you are ashamed of your name, or you feel ridiculed by the fact that I happened to list your name here, well then maybe you need to call yourself something else.

Just keep in mind that nobody is making fun of YOU (the person with the name). We (the writer and the readers of this book) don't know who you are and frankly, we don't care. It's your name, not you, that's funny. We're sure you're a very nice person and nobody is going to think any less of you. Really. There's nothing personal about this: how could it be? We don't know you. Nor do we want to. So don't contact me (the writer). And I mean that sincerely.

With all that being said, here are the names.…

Part 1: Last Name Dick

A. Dick: Hey, what a great way to start a listing: with the basics! Looking for A. Dick? Try the public phone directories in Ganado, AZ; Indian Wells, AZ; Beverly Hills, CA; Colorado Springs, CO; Bridgeport, CT; Raytown, MO; Holly Springs, NC; Brooklyn, NY; Freedom, NY; Warrenton, OR; Arlington, VA; Powhatan, VA; Brattleboro, VT; and Everett, WA. It's good to know that wherever you are, there's A. Dick near you!

*** CELEBRITY DICK ***

Andy Dick: (1965–) Actor, comedian, *The Andy Dick Show, Newsradio,* many other credits.

Anita Dick: Whether you're a man or a woman, it's still true (even if you already have one, you still need it!) Three were found in public phone books: Manhattan, NY; Wabasha, MN; and Welches, OR.

Carrot Dick: This guy should be interviewed. Maybe his is orange? He's listed in the public phone book of Ortonville, MI.

*** LITERARY DICK ***

Deadeye Dick: (1982) Literary character by Kurt Vonnegut.

*** WILD WEST DICK ***

Deadwood Dick: The most famous Black Cowboy. Born Nat Love as a slave in Tennessee, he eventually became an accomplished cowboy. On 4 July 1876, he won a roping and shooting contest in Deadwood, SD; from this point on he was known as Deadwood Dick. For more information on black cowboys, go to www.blackcowboys.com.

Harry Dick: An old joke come to life. He might want to pay a visit to **Dick Barber** (q.v.). Found in the Jeffers, MN public phone book; an unlisted one resides in KS.

Ivana Dick: Another old joke, but what's the truth? According to an internet service that searches public records, the following real people are actually out there, in the following states:

Iva M. Dick, KS
Iva M. Dick, CA
Iva L. Dick, KY
Ivan J. Dick, TX
Ivan R. Dick, MI
Ivan L. Dick, OH
Ivan F. Dick, IL
Ivan C. Dick, WA
Ivan Dick, OR

So whether it's Iva Dick, or Ivan (eye-VON) Dick, they are really out there, but further research will be necessary to confirm whether there is an actual Ivana Dick roaming around, a free-floating joke.

*** LITERARY DICK ***

Moby Dick: The great white whale, of Herman Melville's novel. Probably a sperm whale.

Ophelia Dick: Another classic. Does she exist? There are three different listings in the AOL white pages showing that unlisted numbers exist for the following:

Ophelia Dick, age 32
Ophelia Dick, age 38
Ophelia T. Dick, age 25

A fee is requested to explore public records for these three listings. If you wanna do it, fine. That's not my job.

Worthy of note: there is also an **Ophelia Cox** in Greenville, NC, and two women named **Ophelia Ball**, one in Spring Hill, FL and one in Cleveland, TN; PLUS there are numerous listings in the AOL White Pages for **Ophelia Balls; Ophelia Butt; Ophelia Butts; Ophelia Wang; Ophelia Allnight; Ophelia Plenty; Ophelia Good; Ophelia Wright** (TX, DE, GA, TN and MN); **Ophelia Right; Ophelia Moore** (CA, KY, LA, GA), **Ophelia Opp, Ophelia Goodnight; Ophelia Tomorrow; Ophelia Nextweek; Ophelia Soon**—and there are so many more.

Peter Dick: Means the same backwards and forwards. Found in the Greenwich, CT phone book.

*** SCIENCE FICTION DICK ***

Philip Kindred Dick: (1928–1982) American science fiction writer. Most popular novel: *The Man In The High Castle* (1962).

*** LITERARY DICK ***

Ragged Dick: (1867) Fictional character. "Ragged Dick: or Street Life in New York" was the first of Horatio Alger's "rags to respectability" novels.

Richard Dick: Basically means the same backwards and forwards too. Found in Manhattan phone book. **Dick Dick**??? Oh yes! *See* that listing, below.

Silke Dick: Goes in smooth. Unlisted number in OH. *See,* also: **Dick Silk.**

Silver Dick: *See* **Dick Bland.**

*** CELEBRITY DICK ***

Tim Allen Dick: (1953–) Actor, stand-up comic, star of 1990s sitcom *Home Improvement.* What, you didn't know that Tim Allen's real surname is Dick? Read his book and find out for yourself. You dick.

U. Dick: Well, if you want to throw a random insult out there, just list yourself this way in the phone book. One individual in CA has done this.

Wanda Dick: How much would you pay to be there when she introduces herself to people? (I'll wait a minute while you figure out why that's funny.) And when she gets married, the clergyman will say, "And do you, Wanda Dick…." Boy, I'd pay to be there. If you "Wanda Dick," you can find these ladies in the unlisted number records of AZ, CO, LA, KY, PA, CT, FL, NC, IN, MD, and WI.

Part 2: First Name Dick

Dick Adicks: A real person (listed as Richard), living in FL.

*** SPORTS DICK ***

Dick Advocaat (1947–) Head coach of the Dutch national football team during Euro 2004. Nickname: "The Little General."

Dick Aiken: Not just a name, it's also a symptom. Listed in the phone book in Briston, VT. *See* also **Dick Payne.**

Dick Aikenhead: Ouch. I would *see* **Dick Doctor** for this one. Just one found (as Richard) in NJ.

Dick Allcock: I've heard of All Stars, but this is a team I wish I could qualify for. And so do you. Teammates can be found in the unlisted number records in KY, FL, RI, MS, TX and IL (as Rick or Richard).

Dick Allred: Unless he's been doing nude sunbathing (like **Dick Tanner** [q.v.]), I'd check with a doctor. Guys with this name can be found in the phone books of Soda Springs, ID; Altus, OK; and Huntington, UT.

Dick Anal: I bent over backwards looking through the public records on the internet to find this name for you. One senior citizen in Florida is listed (as Richard) with this name. Be sure not to miss the listing for **Dick Oral** (q.v.).

Dick Angel: I'll bet you didn't even *know* there was a Dick Angel. I'd leave it to your dirty little imagination to think of how he earned his wings. I'm not touching this one with a ten foot **Dick Pole** (q.v.). Fortunately for you, there is a real Dick Angel; according to the public records, there's one living in Cocoa, FL. And there are many more, with unlisted numbers, in several other States.

Dick Apathy: When you just don't give a dick. One guy in FL bears this name (as Richard), but who cares?

*** POLITICAL DICK ***

Dick Armey: Congressman (R-TX), Republican Majority Leader.

Dick Armstrong: What you get from masturbating on a daily basis? Not exactly a problem, mind you, but you only get it on one side. Found in the unlisted records of CA, WA, NM, ID, TX, OK, MN, NE, KY, AL, FL, NC, ME, MA, AZ, GA, UT, PA, DE, and NJ.

Dick Assman: A tough surname to begin with, the chosen moniker guarantees a lifetime of missed opportunities with sensitive people. There are at least 2 of them out there, one in NY, one in MI.

Dick Attorney: Almost goes without saying. With all due respect, of course. But a real Richard Attorney has a listing in CA and FL. *See,* also, **Dick Lawyer; Dick Client.**

Dick Baby: Ewwww. Nasty, nasty thought. Nothing funny about it. And to make it worse, three men out there (as Richard) are in the unlisted number records, in FL, CA and CO with this name.

Dick Bacon: These guys must know how to bring it home. Listings are found for them in OR, CA, NE, CA, WA, WY and WI. This begs the question: is there a Dick Sausage? Sadly, no. But you can have a **Dick Link** (q.v.).

Dick Badcock: Another attention-getting family name, and you have to wonder why anyone whose parents had the blindness (or savage sense of humor) to name them Richard would compound the error by choosing to be known publicly as Dick. My search found just a Richard, in NC, but you know that others are just waiting to be found.

Dick Bagel: I prefer the pumpernickle variety, myself. One guy in California is known by this name. Maybe he likes to have cream cheese spread all over him. Or it. You know, of course, that the most popular man in the nudist colony is the one who can carry five bagels and two cups of coffee. And not to digress too far, but while we're on the subject, the most popular woman at the nudist colony is the one who can eat the fifth bagel.

Dick Bagg: Found in public records only as Richard, but surely their friends call them…. Anyway, this name can be found in CA, FL, NY, NJ, CT, MA, KS and FL directories.

Dick Bald: If you want a bald dick, then skip over the listing for **Dick Hair.** But you might want to visit **Dick Barber** or **Dick Shaver** (q.v.). As you can imagine there are quite a few bald dicks out there, in NY, MO, IL, OH, IA, and CA.

Dick Ball: Somehow the surname Ball passes under the radar when the first name is Lucy, but place a Dick in front of it and all of a sudden you have an entry in a book like this. Men named Dick Ball can be found in public phone directories in Buena Park, CA; Yukon, OK; and Salt Lake City, UT.

Dick Balls: For some reason, Balls impacts on the funny-name radar many times more than the singular Ball, perhaps because testicles are almost never referred to individually. Yet, luckily for you, two Dick Balls are out there for your juvenile titillation: one of these guys is in KS, the other in IL.

Dick Bang: A Fourth of July stunt gone bad? Or some Chinese girl's reference to sexual intercourse? A genuine Dick Bang lives somewhere in CA.

Dick Banger: Any relation to **Dick Pound** (q.v.)? Who knows? A few of them are out there (as Richard) in IA, NY, NC, IL and AZ.

Dick Bangs: The very name spells P-A-R-T-Y! The name also conjures up, perhaps, a gay orgy. But you'll have to go to IA or FL to get it on, because that's where the two gentlemen reside whom I found with this interesting name.

Dick Barber: This is the guy that **Dick Head** goes to for a trim for his **Dick Hair** and maybe his **Dick Beard** (q.v.). Look for the red-white-and-blue striped pole in OR, CA, CO, TX, NE, MT, GA, NC, VA, AK, KS, MI, WV, FL and TN.

Dick Barbie: That's what Ken would do if he weren't gay. AZ and ND are home to two dudes (as Richard) who go by this label.

Dick Beach: It's "where the boys are." It's where you find **Dick Sand** (q.v.). And always found in the company of **Dick Shore** (q.v.). In the public phone books of Wildomar, CA; Ephrata, PA and Marcellus, MI.

Dick Bear: Looks funnier in the phone listing as Bear, Dick. Several people "bear" this name, and they reside in PA, VA, OK, and MI.

Dick Beard: A perfect customer for **Dick Barber** or **Dick Shaver** who could use a **Dick Razor** (q.v.) on him. If you're looking for a Dick Beard or maybe just a dick beard, check the public phone books of Sonora, CA; Margate, FL; Pompano Beach, FL; Decatur, IN; St. Louis, MO; El Reno, OK; Buchanan, VA and Tacoma, WA.

Dick Beaver: On every man's "to do" list. And on the mailboxes of two guys in Huntsville, AL and Blairsden-Graegle, CA.

Dick Bell: As with a cat, hang one of these around its neck so you'll know when it's coming. Where do you find a dick bell? In the public phone books of Desert Hot Springs, CA; Santa Rosa, CA; Valley Ford, CA; San Francisco, CA; Washington, DC; Lake Panasoffkee, FL; Pensacola, FL; Winter Springs, FL; Sanibel, FL; Washington, UT; Amarillo, TX; Ponca City, OK; Portland, OR; Bothell, WA; Wenatchee, MA; Lincoln, NE; Eyota, MN; Afton, IA; Cincinnati, OH; Dothan, AL; Huntsville, AL; Athens, GA; Gainesville, GA; Stockbridge, GA; Gillette, WY; Chase City, VA; and unlisted numbers in WY, PA, AZ, ND and MI.

Dick Bender: A minor collision in the Penismobile? An unusual method of displaying strength? Two fellows by this name were found in public phone books in Terre Haute, IN and Billings, MT.

Dick Beninya: Another one of those names that sounds like a schoolyard joke. And yet, sure enough, somebody by this name has an unlisted number in IL.

Dick Bent: So sorry to hear that. Gentlemen by this name have records in MS and IL. *See,* also, **Dick Dent.**

Dick Berger: Sounds the same as Dick Burger (see below), but we can't vouch for the taste! However, this franchise has more locations: Oxford, AR; Phoenix, AZ; Yuma, AZ; Denver, CO; Garrison, IA; Moscow, ID and Akron, OH.

Dick Berry: Source of the wonderful Dickberry Wine? If you want to pick some Dick Berries, look in Mobile, AL; La Verne, CA; Colorado Springs, CO; Chokoloskee, FL; Xenia, IL; and a bunch of unlisted addresses in IN, KY, LA, ME, MI, NC, OR, TX, WA, WI, VA and GA.

Dick Best: When you see this name in the directories as Best, Dick, it seems more like an advertisement than a person's name. Any way you look at it, it is a name to live up to. And there is a lot of competition! You can find these guys in CA, TX, NE, MO, KY, GA, OH, WI, FL, and WV. Who really has the best dick? Maybe we should ask **Dick Judge** (q.v.).

Dick Bigcock: The public records database shows that there is, indeed, at least one individual in America whose surname is Bigcock. I won't reveal his first name or what State he lives in, because he probably has enough troubles—or inquiries, at least. But alas, no Dicks or Richards are in the listings. *See,* also: **Dick Littlecock.**

Dick Bigg: Bad enough forwards, but when written alphabetically—Bigg, Dick—it's the kind of name you don't want to give to a cop, a nurse, or, certainly, your child's teacher. No wonder this CA resident has an unlisted phone number. I'd like to hear his line when he tries to pick up women.

Dick Bigger: Uh-oh. There's a challenge for Mr. Bigg. Get out the tape measure. Just one listing, in IL. And that's enough, if you ask me.

Dick Biggs: Great name for a porno star, bad name otherwise. Just one found, located in Camarillo, CA.

Dick Biter: It's not just an insult, it's a name! At least 6 (as Richard) are living with unlisted numbers in OK, MD, PA, GA, FL and MI.

Dick Black: Innocuous enough looking until you see it listed in public phone books as BLACK, DICK. These colorful gentlemen can be found in Farley, IA; Helena, MT; Wellfleet, NE; Eugene, OR; Buckeye, AZ; Denver, CO; and some other locations.

Dick Blackcock: A great name, and it does exist as a genuine surname, but there are no Dicks or Richards found in the database. *See,* also: **Dick Whitecock.**

Dick Bland: For those on a bland diet, I guess. Three men were found with this name, in Hilton Head Island, SC; Bryan, OH; and Fenton, MO. [Historical note: U.S. Senator Richard P. Bland (D-Missouri), who served from 1873–1894, was known as Silver Dick because of his relentless stance for the free coinage of silver (thus increasing the supply of money into the marketplace and giving Western silver mine owners guaranteed sales to the U.S. Mint).]

Dick Blocker: A birth control device? Also a good name for a lesbian. One guy with this name is indicated as living in GA.

Dick Blood: Major symptom of a damaged kidney. Seek medical attention immediately or call **Dick Doctor** (q.v.). A singularly unattractive name, to say the least. At least two, and possibly four, individuals with unlisted phone numbers are in the records as residing in TX and ME.

Dick Blowers: Isn't it nice to know that instead of dating a girl for a while to find out if she's one of these, you can just look them up in the phone book? One gentleman with this name is found in WI, but as "Richard" they can be found in CA, MO, MN, FL, NC, NY, WA, MI, TX and IA.

Dick Blown: Mission accomplished? Several specimens of this name (as Richard) can be found in NY and WI. Lucky guys.

Dick Blue: I would expect each one to have a flat-screen TV built into the head. You can fly Dick Blue—if he says ok—in FL, IN, WI, TX, NC, and WA.

Dick Booger: Just one more name for a load? There is one in the record books, as Richard, in Florida.

Dick Boring: Don't yawn too wide, you don't know what he's capable of. He's in OH if you care to find him.

Dick Boner: A hard man to locate. He has an unlisted number in California.

Dick Boss: Aren't they all? There are at least 4 guys with this name, two in MA, two in OH. But how many *deserve* this name? Ho ho, that's a whole 'nother book.

Dick Bottoms: Sounds like fun. Unless you're on the bottom. I mean, I wouldn't know, but I've heard so much about it. *You* probably know. Especially if you've done much traveling in the Middle East. But I hear it can hurt. Sometimes. Did you see *Deliverance*? Anyway, it goes on (under the name Richard, only) in CA, OK, KS, KY (that's it…use KY!), TN, NC, VA, ME, TX, MO, FL, AZ, ME, NJ, NV, MA, ID, NY, PA, LA, and OR.

Dick Box: A sport? Or a part of the anatomy? It's for you to wonder about. Two of them are out there and they are in TX and WA.

Dick Boxer: I've heard of kick boxing, but this sounds more painful. AOL white pages show at least three of these guys with unlisted phone numbers.

Dick Bra: I didn't even know they *made* such a thing! And yet there they are, in the public records (as Richard) with unlisted numbers in CA, FL, MA, IN, NC, AR and LA. I guess you only need one of these if you're a **Dick Hung** (q.v.).

Dick Brace: Good for sprains, although I'm not sure how you would get an injury like that. Oh wait, I guess I can. Listed in the public phone book in Campton, NH.

Dick Bragg: A guy who claims to be **Dick Best** (q.v.)? You would expect to find these men everywhere (if you're female, you've probably met at least one!) but according to the unlisted phone records they are actually in KY, NC, WV, ME, and IN.

Dick Brain: A real name, although it really shouldn't be, and there are two guys out there that can be found in OR and TX.

Dick Brest: The name "Breast" exists as a family name, but I could not find any Dicks or Richards listed. But with this spelling, there is one Richard in Ohio. Dick Brest sounds like a fun activity.

Dick Breath: "No!" you cry out. "There simply cannot be anybody who is actually named Dick Breath!" You're wrong. He's out there. The internet public records show that there is one such person, and he lives in WI. Now, wasn't that alone worth the price of this book?

Dick Bridges: These help us pass over the rivers and other obstacles that we encounter in life. Yeah, right. The Bay Bridge is in San Francisco and the Narrows Bridge is in New York, but to find Dick Bridges you have to look in Arkadelphia, AR; Douglasville, GA; Dubuque, IA; Saint Ann, MO; and Grapeland, TX. *See also* **Dick Steele.**

Dick Broad: Read forwards or backwards, it's good. One man in NE is found in the public records with this name.

Dick Brothers: Wasn't that a movie with John Holmes and Ron Jeremy? Or is this what they do in Arkansas? You can find these guys in the public phone books of Washington, IN and Manhattan, KS. For a "related" entry, *see,* also: **Dick Sisters.**

Dick Brush: Do you use one of these to keep your dick well groomed? **Dick Head** (q.v.) uses it on his **Dick Hair** (q.v.). This name shows up in Pekin, IL and Greenville, NY.

Dick Bull: This has to be one of the toughest macho names in the world. I'd like to be called Dick Bull. This sounds like a guy who can punch a hole through your car door with his fist. If I ever write a screenplay with a tough guy character in it, he's gonna be called Dick Bull. Or **Dick Hammer** (q.v.). A few Dick Bulls are out there, all in NE and OR, and I wouldn't want to get them angry. *See,* also: **Dick Cow.**

Dick Bullet: Who better to stick into **Dick Gunn** (q.v.)? There are two guys out there in the unlisted phone records with this name (as Richard), in PA and CA.

Dick Burger: Hold my pickle! And watch out for that Special Sauce! Today in America you can only find Dick Burgers in Oakhurst, CA and Lexington, IL. *See also* **Dick Berger**, above.

Dick Burns:. I saw, to my regret, a video clip on www.bangedup.com that shows exactly how somebody might sustain such an injury. Despite the unpleasant mental image produced by the name, 17 such individuals were found in public phone books, including Colorado Springs, CO; Melbourne, FL; Cotati, CA, Kings Beach CA; Sarasota FL; Archer IA; DesMoines, IA; Aledo, IL; Mankato, KA; Pequot Lakes, MN; Woodstock, NH; Houston, TX; and Rockdale, TX. *See also* **Dick Flaming.**

Dick Bush: Democratic campaign slogan? These politically-challenged gentlemen can be found in the phone books of Burney, CA; Aurora, CO; Decatur, IL; Sterling Heights, MI; Fort Worth, TX; Irving TX; and Morrison, IL.

Dick Buss: All aboard! Next stop: Intercourse, Pennsylvania! Two men with this name are in the unlisted records of OH and IA. And of course, every **Dick Buss** has a **Dick Driver** (q.v.).

*** CELEBRITY DICK ***

Dick Butkus: (1942–) One of the greatest linebackers to ever play professional football. He played his entire career with the Chicago Bears. Elected to the Pro Football Hall of Fame in 1979.

Dick Butter: This is what you get when you churn the **Dick Cream** (q.v.) There are a bunch of Richard Butters out there, in PA, FL, MN, NJ, and MI.

*** CELEBRITY DICK ***

Dick Button: (1929–) Pro Figure Skater. Five time World Champion, two Olympic Gold Medals.

Dick Butts: An apt name if your forte is performing anal sex, but otherwise probably a liability. Despite this, 5 listings for this name are in public phone books, four in Ohio, one in Florida.

Dick Candy: Not suitable for children. Careful not to take any from strangers. One guy with this name is listed in MS.

Dick Carpenter: These are the guys who works with **Dick Wood** (q.v.). You can find them in Fairfield Bay, AR; Mesa, AZ; La Quinta, CA; Valencia, CA; Whitethorn, CA; Arvada, CO; Colorado Springs, CO; Peyton, CO; Woodland Park, CO; Stanford, KY; Cedar Springs, MI; Aztec, NM; Farmington, NM; Las Vegas, NV; Stamford, NY; West Mansfield, OH; Coulee Dam, WA; Okaogan, WA; Spokane, WA; Hillsdale, MI; Rochester, MN; Flint, MI; Flushing, MI; Petal, MS; and Marysville, WA.

Dick Carr: A Mercedes, a Porche, a Corvette, and just about any car that guys buy to "compensate." And of course every **Dick Carr** has a **Dick Driver** (q.v.).

*** HOLLYWOOD DICK ***

Dick Carson: (1929–) TV producer: *Get Smart, Wheel of Fortune, The Merv Griffin Show, The Tonight Show.*

*** CELEBRITY DICK ***

Dick Cavett: Host, *The Dick Cavett Show,* 1969–1972, very hip late-night talk show (Jimi Hendrix and Janis Joplin, among others, appeared as guests).

Dick Challenger: Entrant in a dick contest? Just three found in the unlisted number records (as Richard), in PA, OH and SC. And if you're wondering if there's a **Dick Contest** out there.... sorry.

Dick Charger: You should always have two: one in your house, and one in your car, so you don't run out of **Dick Power** (q.v.). The only trouble is, Dick Chargers are very hard to find: there's only one in the records (under Richard) in CT.

Dick Chaser: There's girls like these in every crowd. And in the phone books! Two, at least (under Richard) in OH and PA.

Dick Cheese: Who would go through life with a name synonymous with smegma? To find out, you might want to contact this individual living in IL; also, Richard Cheese is a novelty song singer (a la Weird Al Yankovic) who performs in lounges. Don't miss our listings for **Dick Milk** and **Dick Cream.** Also, *see* **Dick Maus.**

*** POLITICAL DICK ***

Dick Cheney: Vice-President of the United States, two terms, 2000–2004 and 2004–2008. Despite being a Republican and standard bearer for that party which is largely influenced by very stiff-necked elements, Cheney had the guts—and the integrity—to publicly announce his love for his lesbian daughter.

Dick Cherry: What used to happen a lot on Prom Night but nowadays occurs way too often before the Sweet Sixteen party. It happens everywhere but as far as public records go, they are shown in UT, MD, MO, AZ, TN, TX, VA, NC, IA, and PA.

Dick Child: The accusation against Michael Jackson? Not the best name in the world to have, and yet at least two guys, one in UT and one in VA, are listed this way.

Dick Chocolate: Comes in White, Milk and Dark. Find these yummy guys in the unlisted records of CT and NJ. *See,* also: **Dick Vanilla, Dick Cherry,** and **Dick Strawberry.**

Dick Church: Services held nightly. Kneeling required. Found in public phone directories in Walpole, ME; Anoka, MN; Greene, NY; Big Sandy, TX; King George, VA; Anacortes, WA and Royal Oak, MI. See also **Dick Temple,** depending on your particular persuasion.

*** CELEBRITY DICK ***

Dick Clark: (1930–) Legendary host of *American Bandstand*, the TV show which launched the careers of countless rock-n-roll bands. Host of *Dick Clark's Rockin' New Year's Eve* annual TV special since 1973.

Dick Client: The source of income for **Dick Lawyer** (q.v.)? One guy in Maryland with this moniker.

Dick Cockburn: Maybe he once sang "Come on baby light my fire" to the wrong girl? I don't know. But I wish him the best. One very old man in MO is listed with this name, and to you, sir, I doff my hat.

Dick Cocker: I wish this guy could get elected President just so that we could hear his name on television every day. Just one brave gentleman is in the public directories with this name, in Carlyle, IL.

Dick Cocks: This is a surname that will either break you or make you tough. And if your parents name you Dick, you probably have to become either a Special Forces soldier or a serial killer. The name has at least three different unlisted number references in AOL white pages.

Dick Coffee: Start your morning right—and hers. And don't forget to add **Dick Cream** (q.v.) and **Dick Sugar.** If you're looking for Dick Coffee, he's in Birmingham, AL.

Dick Coffin: After **Dick Death** (q.v.) occurs, you'll need one of these. You can find them in CA, ME, and OR.

Dick Cola: It's the real thing! You can find them (as Richard) in OH, PA, MA; NJ; CA and MD.

Dick Comer: Anybody with this name, you don't want to rub the wrong way. Unless you're wearing a raincoat. You can find these guys in the phone books of Waukee, IA; Union City, IN; Boone, NC; and Coal Grove, OH.

*** MUSICAL DICK ***

Dick Contino: (1930–) "World's Greatest Accordionist." Has sold over 6 million records. Made a record number of appearances on the *Ed Sullivan Show*. He was a huge star in his heyday. When is the last time you saw somebody play the accordion? And can you visualize any song at all being played on it, except for *Lady of Spain?*

Dick Cook: Does he start with **Dick Raw** to make **Dick Tartar** (q.v.)? I shudder to think what he stirs the **Dick Soup** (q.v.) with. If you get the urge, look in the unlisted records in WA, CA, OR, NV, ID and AZ.

Dick Cool: Yeah, baby! Shagadelic! Who wouldn't like to be called Dick Cool? And there's a few of them out there, in Waterloo, IA; and unlisted locations in OH and MN. *See*, also: **Dick Kool.**

Dick Coon: Coon Dick? I've heard of a coonskin cap, but...wait, is that the thing that hangs from the cap? Found in the public records of WA, CA, MN, ME and PA.

Dick Copp: This must be who enforces the **Dick Law** (q.v.). Found only in Independence, MO.

Dick Cotton: Natural fibers are always more comfortable, and of course they breathe, keeping you cooler in the summer. They may shrink, though, which can be a disadvantage. Looking for Dick Cotton? Peruse the public phone books in Glasgow, MT and Emory, TX.

Dick Cousins: I guess it's all relative. You'd expect them in Arkansas, but they are listed only in VA, NJ and ME. Oh, and be sure to use a condom. You know what the kids are like when cousins do it.

Dick Cow: A guy who mates with **Dick Bull** (q.v.)? There are about six Dick Cows in the unlisted records (as Richard) in NY, CA, GA, TN and OR.

Dick Cox: Another porno star name. Incredibly, I found 21 of them in public phone books from Sitka, AK to Lumberton NC.

Dick Cranium: I wouldn't have thought that "Cranium" was a real name, but strangely enough there are a bunch of them out there, in UT, OR, FL, DE, AR, FL, CA, NJ, OH, GA and MN.

Dick Craven: Girls, you've had this from time to time, right? Craven, Dick? Well, satisfy your "craven" in LaSalle, CO; Windsor Heights, IA; Denton, TX; Provo, UT; Long Beach, CA; Bellevue, WA; and Renton, WA.

Dick Cream: What you see at the end of every porno flick ever made. For people with this cinematic name, look (as Richard) in CA, NJ, AL, PA and CT. The perfect complement to your **Dick Coffee** (q.v.). *See*, also, **Dick Milk** and **Dick Cheese**, because we carry a complete selection of dairy products.

Dick Creamer: Uh, no thanks, I prefer half-and-half in my coffee. Seven of these guys can be found in TX, IA, and AL.

Dick Crisp: Nobody wants soggy dick, right? This variety can be found only in WI.

Dick Crotch: I was almost a little surprised when I could not find a Dick Crotch anywhere in the public records, nor even a Richard. However, Crotch is indeed a family name, with numerous members listed around the country, including, for your juvenile amusement, one **Harry Crotch** residing in Puerto Rico and another by the same name in PA.

Dick Crumb: Lives in MN. Alone, most likely.

Dick Cumming: How can you have a conversation with a guy with this name, or about him, and keep a straight face? "I'd like to introduce you all to our new Human Resources director, Dick Cumming." Hard to conceive. Or maybe that's a poor choice of words. Anyway, there are listings for this name in NE and FL.

Dick Cummings: That's what you can find all over hotel bedspreads with an ultraviolet light. They can also be found living in CA, OH, TN, PA, MA, IA, TX, MD, OH, and NV (and, as a side note, **Ophelia Cummings** is listed in NC, OH, NY, LA, and IA).

Dick Cunty: Well, there are no Dick Cuntys, nor Richard Cuntys, found anywhere in the public phone directories, or indicated as unlisted in the non-public references. However, Cunty, it turns out, is a real family surname, with seven individuals residing in six states under—understandably—unlisted numbers, so that idiots don't bother them with crank phone calls. One can only imagine how difficult it is to convince a woman to marry you if that's your last name.

Dick Curley: Looks even better in the phone book as **Curley, Dick.** Hope everything straightens out for these two guys in CA and AZ. *See,* also: **Dick Strait.** Say, if Dick Curley were to go into business with **Dick Short** (q.v.), they could call themselves **Short & Curley.**

Dick Curry: You'd have to search a lot of Indian restaurants to find this exotic treat. You might start with the public phone books in Cookeville, TN; Old Hickory, TN; Springtown, TX; Long Beach, WA; and Buckhannon, WV.

Dick Cutter: Uh, oh. Is this Lorena Bobbit using an assumed name? This real listing is in CA and I would steer clear of it.

Dick Daily: Sounds like a prescription for a good time. They are found in OK, UT, OR, UT (one listing for "**Dick M. Daily**") *see also* **Dick Daley.** Either way, somebody's happy.

*** MUSICAL DICK ***

Dick Dale: "The King of the Surf Guitars." Dale invented surf music in the 1950s. His 1961 hit *Let's Go Trippin* was released a month before the Beach Boys' *Surfin'*. Inducted into the Surfing Hall of Fame, 1989. The Fender guitar company makes a Dick Dale Signature Stratocaster. Dick is still playing and recording; in 2004 he released a new CD, *Spacial Disorientation.* For more information go to www.dickdale.com.

Dick Daley: Even easier to find than the Daily variety, with listings in MA, MO, ME, CA, ID, and PA.

Dick Danger: This is the sign hanging from the waist of **Dick Monster** (q.v.). Maybe. Either that or a private eye who investigates sex crimes. You can find these adventurous men in just two listings: CA and FL.

*** CARTOON DICK ***

Dick Dastardly: Cartoon character from Saturday-morning TV show *The Wacky Races* (1968). With his doggy companion Muttley, this Dick tried to cheat in every conceivable way, but always lost in the end.

Dick Death: When **Dick Doctor**'s (q.v.) best efforts fail, this is the tragic result. Fortunately, Dick Death (listed only as Richard) occurs only in CA, WA, ID and VA. For possible causes, *see* **Dick Burns** and **Dick Green.** And if this happens, you'll need a **Dick Coffin** (q.v.).

Dick DeFace: Sounds like a plan. Several listings in TX (as Richard) for this singular name. Worth a mention: Peter DeFace, found in FL.

Dick Delight: And I couldn't agree more. There is apparently one such person, living in CA.

Dick Demento: CA, FL and NC are home to at least three gentlemen by this name (as Richard). What are the chances that at least one of them is known as "Crazy Dick"?

Dick DeMouth: You don't just find names like these. You have to look for them. According to the AOL white pages, there are three different individuals with this name: Dick A. DeMouth; Dick S. DeMouth; and Dick DeMouth (sorry, there is no Dick N. DeMouth, which would have been almost.... too perfect). DeMouth is a genuine family surname, I have learned, with several members in two different States.

Dick Dent: When dicks collide, this is what can happen. But a little Bondo and some sandpaper, and it should look like new. If you want to find a Dick Dent, there's one in Houston, TX. *See*, also, **Dick Bent.**

Dick Diaz: Any relation to **Dick Bottoms** (q.v.)? We don't know. One public phone listing (as Dickie) in El Paso, TX. Hundreds of listings as Richard. But anybody named Richard N. Diaz can fairly be called **Dick N. Diaz,** for your silly entertainment, and those can be found in TX, CO, CA, FL and OK.

Dick Dick: Even if your first name is Richard, and your last name is Dick, why on earth would you choose not only to call yourself Dick, but to use it as your official name for all your records? And it isn't just *one* guy, it's a *whole bunch* of them. You don't believe it? Look it up yourself: Guys with this name are listed in OR, AZ, TX, KS (several of them, with different middle names), MO, FL, NY (several), CA, IN, MA, MI, AZ, WA, IA, ID, ND, MN and AR.

Incidentally, a *dik-dik* is a type of African antelope. One of the smallest antelopes, dik-diks live in dense wooded areas. Four species live in eastern Africa and one in southwestern Africa. The tallest dik-diks are about 15 inches (40 centimeters) high at the shoulder. Females are larger than males but have no horns. Dik-diksare delicate, slender animals with tiny hoofs, short tails, and long, hairy muzzles. They live alone or in groups of two or three. Dik-diks warn each other of danger with high-pitched whistles. Dik-diks belong to the bovid family, Bovidae. They are genus *Madoqua*. This concludes the intellectual and socially-redeeming section of this book.

Dick Dicker: Well, if there is Dumb and Dumber, why not? Believe it or not, this is a name belonging to two guys, one in WA, one in CA.

Dick Dinner: OK, no Dicks out there, technically, but several Richards in CA, which is good enough for me. I've served a few dick dinners in my day; so have you, I'll bet. Or been served, as the case may be.

Dick Doctor: To maintain **Dick Health** (q.v.), you'd be smart to see one of these guys at least once a year, or when any of the symptoms described elsewhere in this book appear. Fortunately, Dick Doctors (listed as Richard) can be found in CA, MO, IL, MI, OH, FL, SC, NC, KS, NY, PA, NJ, IL, WA, and MA.

Dick Dogg: Sounds pretty cool, actually, if you're a rapper or gangbanger. Could be tough to get into medical school, though. Another CA-only find.

Dick Doody: Too scatalogical for me. Maybe it's more *your* speed. One gentleman in CA calls this name his own.

Dick Dragon: These fire-breathing monsters can be found in Indiana and Nevada. But they'd better be careful that they don't run into **Dick Slayer** or **Dick Knight** (q.v.).

Dick Drinkwater: Now *there's* an act I would like to see. But I would have to go to either VA or SC to see it. Many more, as Richard, are scattered all over the country.

Dick Driver: They can take you to some interesting places, ladies, in a long, pink (or black) limousine. Or in a **Dick Buss** (q.v.). If you want to find these special chauffeurs, they live in AL, WA and NC. *See,* also: **Dick Carr.**

Dick Dumass: No. Couldn't find one. Even though this surname is properly pronounced "doo-MAAHS," and not "dumb-ass" (remember that great beer commercial with the guy on the job interview?), it still would have been funny—in a retarded sort of way—if there was a Dick Dumass out there. Not being easily deterred, I searched for, and found, several **Dick Dumas's** out there, but only a dumbass would pronounce Dumas as "dumb ass" and so I have not included those references in this book.

Dick Duncan: Sounds like a euphemism for sexual intercourse. "Mmm-hmm, I did some heavy dick duncan last night!" Quite a few of them out there, too: in WA, OR, CO, OK, MO, IA, KY, GA and AR.

Dick Dunn: Have you Dunn, Dick? These guys have: AK, WA, WY, CO, TX, MO, WI, IA, MI, AL, FL, GA, NC, PA, CT, VT, WA, OK, ID, OH, MI, MA, OR and IN.

*** POLITICAL DICK ***

Dick Durbin: (1944–) Democratic Senator from Illinois. He is the Minority Whip, which means he is the Assistant Minority Leader (the Democrats are currently the minority party in Congress). But Minority Whip sounds like what the slaveowners used to do.

Dick Dyke: That's what guys fantasize about when they watch lesbian scenes in porno flicks. One lucky guy is listed this way in the phone book of Jenison, MI.

Dick Eaton: Looks much funnier in the phone book, where it says Eaton, Dick. Have you been to a Dick Eaton contest? If not, try looking in OR, TX, FL, ME, MO, MA, OK, ID and MI.

Dick Economy: This is the one to buy when you can't afford that high-priced dick. Three listings for this name, all in CA. *See*, also, **Dick Price, Dick Money, Dick Giant.**

Dick Elefant: AOL's white pages show at least three ELEFANT, DICKs with unlisted numbers. You've watched Animal Planet, haven't you....? You'd have to have special pants made for you.

*** SPORTS DICK ***

Dick Enberg: (1935–) CBS sportscaster.

Dick Enright: If you've got your Dick Enright, she'll appreciate it. You can find your Dick Enright in the public phone books of Sun City, AZ and Sioux Falls, SD.

Dick Eye: Some sort of opthomological disorder? There's a man in PA with this name.

Dick Eyer: A guy who spends way too much time in the public men's room? Found one in PA. Maybe he knows **Dick Eye** (q.v.).

Dick Face: Lives in MI. Alone, I'm guessing. And very, very bitter. Sometimes seen in the company of **Dick Shaver** (q.v.).

Dick Factor: You've heard of The O'Reilly Factor; maybe this is a political talk show about Dicks. Or is The Dick Factor the phenomenon that explains why men behave the way they do? If you're looking for Dick Factor, they have unlisted numbers (as Richard) in TX, MN, OH, NJ, RI, and MA.

Dick Fagg: I was searching for **Dick Faggot,** but I was disappointed to find none—not even a Richard. Although I did discover that Faggot is a real family name, with people out there using it every day. Not a lot of people, as you might expect, but a few of them. But while I was searching for them, I did find a Dick Fagg, just one, living in MO (which is kind of appropriate).

Dick Fairy: I don't even want to *think* about what he might leave under your pillow—or why. Just one listing (as Richard) in PA.

Dick Fake: Prosthesis? Dildo? Old Maid's Friend? Lesbian in-line connector? I know that I would not want my name listed in any record as "Fake, Dick." And yet, two gentlemen in New York do. And there are many more, as Richard, in CO, PA, AZ, CA and WY.

Dick Farmer: What kind of seed do you plant to get…. oh. Never mind. True to America's agricultural heritage, Dick Farmers can be found in NV, TX, AZ, KS, IL, OH, GA, SC, AR, IA, TN, AZ and PA.

Dick Farter: Oh, come on now, you say. Don't tell me that there are really people out there with the surname *Farter*. Listen: I wouldn't list it here unless it was really out there in the public records available on the internet. Richard Farter is listed as living in CO. Hopefully, not near any open flames.

Dick Fast: Is this a voluntary abstention from dick? Or is it a morning meal for lovers? Or just competition for **Dick Quick** (q.v.)? You can find out for yourself by checking the public phone listings in St. Augustine, FL and Big Sky, MT. If this isn't your speed, *see* **Dick Slow.**

Dick Fatt: Have you been looking for a Fatt, Dick? Or have you ever called someone a fat dick? Well, the chances are only about 1 in 125 million that you literally got it right. Dick Fatt (as Richard) can be found in NY, FL and CA. An alternate spelling, **Dick Fat**, belongs to several *entirely different* gentlemen (as Richard) in GA, AZ, and MI.

While we're on the subject, let me digress a bit to point out that there is a **Fat Wang** in the public phone book of San Francisco, and several **Fat Wong**s in New York and California phone listings.

Dick Feeder: Another name for Purina Dick Chow? Or is that the dispenser for the dick chow? We don't want to know. But there are several Richard Feeders out there, in CA, TN, IL, IN, FL, and IA. Bon appetit.

Dick Ferry: Is this the boat you take to get to Neverland? I don't wanna find out. If you do, you can find them in NY, CA and OR.

Dick Fester: Is this the one member of The Addams Family that they couldn't show on television? I would hate to see his…"Thing." There are some festering dicks out there with unlisted numbers (as Richard) in NY, TN, MI, PA, MO, VA and MA.

*** CELEBRITY DICK ***

Dick Fick: (1953–) The former college basketball coach at Morehead State University. The Dick Fick Award is named after him.

Dick Field: Subject of the movie, *Field of Dicks*? If you build it, they will come. So have plenty of Kleenex. If you're looking for Dick Field, they're in the public phone books of Sun City, AZ; Escondito, CA; Hungry Horse, MT; and Bridgeport, WA.

Dick Fiend: Some people just can't get enough of it, so I guess they turn into this. Two of them are out there, with unlisted numbers (as Richard) in NY and OH. You might prefer **Dick Friend** (q.v.).

Dick Finder: Most guys can do this without any help (check between your belly button and your knees), but if you need help, call on one of these gentlemen, with unlisted numbers in WA and CA (as Richard).

Dick Fine: If you're looking for Fine, Dick, check the phone books in Gunnison, CO; Pueblo, CO; and unlisted numbers in CA and GA.

Dick Finger: A bad James Bond flick? It sure looks bad in the listing as Finger, Dick. Look in OR, AZ, CA GA and TN for the poor souls with this name.

Dick Fink: A name that just doesn't roll mellifluously off the tongue. Several guys by this name are in the unpublished listings for NE, MI, WA, MN, FL, and IN.

Dick First: And ask questions later. Like, "What's your name?" maybe. One fella in Wyoming is listed with this name.

Dick Fisher: If you're going dick fishing, may I suggest that for bait you use lipstick, a tight skirt and a wonderbra. And if you're going dick fishing, bring a buddy. You can find them in the phone books of Tuscon, AZ; Rancho Mirage, CA; Kissimmee, FL; Pensacola, FL; Losantville, IN; Chandler, AZ; Sacramento, CA; Eden Prairie, MN; Boulder, CO; Denver, CO; Shell Knob, MO; Monticello, IN; Smithville, MO; Fort Benton, MT; Burlington, NC; Gastonia, NC; Fremont, NE; Oklahoma City, OK; Halsey, NE; Gold Hill, OR; Ooltewah, TN; San Benito, TX; Tooele, UT; Burlington, VT; Spokane, WA; Powell, WY; Muskegon, MI, Kenna, WV; Torrance, CA; Minneapolis, MN; Beaverton, OR; Wapakoneta, WI; and Bridgewater, NJ. And you might want to bring **Dick Worm** (q.v.).

Dick Fitzgood: Somebody's happy in *his* house—listed in IN.

Dick Fitzwell: Now there's a contented man. And wife. Several, actually: listings are found in WI, CA, OK, MI, PA, MD, and FL.

Dick Flaming: I'm sure I've met this one. So have you. We've all known some flaming dicks. Or is that a dessert at the Cannibal Café? But there has to be more than just this one guy located in KS.

Dick Flash: A nice day in the park. Sitting on a bench having lunch. Mothers with strollers. Kids on the swings. Along comes a man wearing a raincoat…seems a bit odd for a sunny day. His head seems tucked into his chest. He's coming closer. Suddenly he yanks open his raincoat with both hands. Dick flash!!

That brings a joke to mind: Three old ladies are sitting on a park bench. A guy in a raincoat comes up and exposes himself. The first old lady had a stroke. The second old lady had a stroke. The third old lady couldn't reach it.

A few guys by this name (as Richard) are found in CA and FL.

Dick Float: Do you know how to make a Dick Float? Two scoops of ice cream, a tablespoon of chocolate syrup, 8 ounces of soda water and a dick. There seems to be just one gentleman out there with this name (as Richard) in FL.

Dick Flood: The end of a porno movie? Or a the result of the breaching of a **Dick Dyke** (q.v.)? Found in IL, FL, NV, WI, GA, CO, KY, NY, and CA unlisted records.

Dick Flower: Well, if a cactus can flower, why not? Belongs to a RI man.

Dick Floyd: Lesser-known psychedelic rock group that put out such minor hits as *Dark Side of My Balls* and *Another Prick In The Wall.* Also, *see* **Dick Pink.** Today, three guys with this name can be found in the public phone listings in Van Buren, AR; Fountain Hills, AZ; and Forsyth, IL.

Dick Flushing: A method for cleaning out clogged dicks? There's one such man in NY with an unlisted number.

Dick Foe: You need a **Dick Friend** to help protect you from these. Fortunately, there is some indication of where these guys are so you can try to avoid them. Several have unlisted numbers (as Richard) in AZ and CO.

Dick Fokker: Surprisingly, none found. There are actually several Gaylord Fokkers, though, in NY, OH and TX, if you're interested (you DO know that name from *Meet The Parents* and *Meet The Fokkers,* don't you?).

Dick Foot: Lesser-known legendary hairy mountain-dwelling monster, only seen in blurry videos. He leaves quite a unique set of tracks; hence the name. While many debate his existence and some swear they have sighted him, I seem to have found him in the public records as having an unlisted phone number in TN.

Dick Force: May this Force be with you. Or a great name for a porno flick about horny cops. These guys can be found in both WV and UT with unlisted numbers.

Dick Foreskin: Oh, you'd just *love* it if there was a guy out there named Dick Foreskin, wouldn't you? Well, guess what: there isn't. Not a Richard, either. But…. there are *five people* in the records with the last name Foreskin, and they live in *five different States* (is one Foreskin all that a single State can handle?). While we're on the subject, **Forskin** is also a real family surname, with quite a few members out there (no pun intended), but again, no Dicks or Richards. Life is full of little disappointments.

Dick Forget: Forget dick? Is this what the spiteful husband says? Or is this what the dick with Alzheimer's says a lot? Either way, it's quite a name, and quite a few guys have it (as Richard) according to the unlisted number records of MI, NY, RI and MA.

Dick Fork: Part of a cannibal's silverware set? You know, along with the salad fork and serving fork? Ask the one fellow (as Richard) in CA who is called by this interesting name.

Dick Forrest: These guys should look up Dick Shaver (and so should you, below). They're located in AK, NM, NC, CA, OR, and CA (and there's a **Dick Forest** in CA—maybe near Sausalito?).

Dick Freedom: Were these guys formerly known as **Dick French** (q.v.) before 9/11? Let dick freedom ring!—by ringing the **Dick Bell** (q.v.), perhaps? Unlisted phone numbers are found for these residents of OH, CT, NY and OR.

Dick French: Candidate for a French kiss? In this post-9/11 world, these guys should change their names to **Dick Freedom** (q.v.). Unlisted numbers in OR, CA, TX, CO, AZ, KS, MI, IN, FL, NY, NH, MO, WA, NV, AL, MN and LA. An amusing variation on this name is a listing for **Dickson D. French,** a resident of KS.

Dick Fresh: Be sure to check the date on the zipper before you open it. And do not purchase if the button is up. Look for fresh dick in your grocer's freezer (as Richard) in CA, OH, OR, TX, WA, UT, and KS.

Dick Friend: Everybody needs one of these. Boy friend, girl friend...dick friend! You can find one in the public phone listings in Hastings, NE; Lakewood, CA; Oakland, MD and Plainfield, IN. But just as we have dick friends in life, we sometimes come across.... a **Dick Foe** (q.v.). *See,* also: **Dick Fiend.**

Dick Fucker: Well, when I searched for this name, I really, really expected the result to be "none found," but I tell ya, I'll be dipped in sheep shit if there aren't two different Richard Fuckers in the unlisted phone records...a Richard J. Fucker in NY and a Richard L. Fucker in MD. I can't even joke about it. I will leave that to people with lower standards than I have.

Dick Fugger: Wouldn't you know it, the family name Fugger has quite a few members out there in this great land of ours, and there is a Richard in Illinois. To him, we tip our hats. Let's just hope that his mom, and the other moms with this name, are not known as Mother Fugger.

Dick Funk: Remember that roommate who didn't shower very often? This is what he had. Among other things. There are a few guys in America with this attractive name, all in CO and NY—to the relief of the other 48 States.

Dick Furry: I hope this guy is a Muppet. He's hiding in MO.

Dick Gardener: Is this the guy who raised **Dick Rose** (q.v.)? And who cultivated **Dick Plant** (q.v.)? And who constantly struggles with **Dick Weed** (q.v.)? Just one man goes by this name, and he's in CA.

*** SCOTTISH DICK ***

Dick Gaughan (1948–) First and foremost, as he says, he is a Scot. And don't forget it. He is a musician, most accomplished on the acoustic guitar, playing jazz and rock but specializing in Scottish and Celtic music. He says his greatest influences were Karl Marx and Groucho Marx.

*** CELEBRITY DICK ***

Dick Gautier: (1937–) Multitalented actor, artist, and personality with a long resume of TV and movie appearances. He was Hymie The Robot on *Get Smart;* he guest starred on *The Mary Tyler Moore Show, The Munsters, Quincy, The Rockford Files, Columbo* and many others. He appeared on Broadway in *Bye Bye Birdie* (Tony nomination); *The Music Man; South Pacific; Cabaret; I Do, I Do;* and lots of other stuff.

Dick Gay: Listed in phone books as GAY, DICK: Ilion, NY; Hendersonville, TN.

Dick Genius: Well, that's *one* way to upstage **Dick Smart** (q.v.). Richard Genius is located in IL. For contrast, *see* **Dick Moron.** How much would you give to see those three guys compete on *Jeopardy?*

*** POLITICAL DICK ***

Dick Gephardt: (1941–) U.S. Congressman (D-MO), former House Majority leader, then House Minority Leader. Candidate for U.S. Presidency, 2004, until he withdrew from the race.

Dick Geyser: The end of every porn movie, and the end of a lot of dates, as far as the guy is concerned. Six States are home to fellows with this name (as Richard): CA, OH, NY, PA, TX and WI.

Dick Giant: If you're looking for Giant, Dick, there are three unlisted ones (as Richard, only) in NY, IN and TX. If saving money is your aim, *see*, also, **Dick Economy, Dick Money.**

Dick Glass: Listed as Glass, Dick, of course—careful—lovely to look at, delightful to hold, but if you break it, consider it sold—found in CA, TX, SC, MS (and honorable mention to Dickson Glass, found in VT and CT).

Dick Glasscock: Handle with care. Two guys, in KY and NJ, and they sound like they need a cast iron jockstrap.

Dick Glazier: When you break a **Dick Glass**, or you're building a **Dick House** (q.v.), you need to call one of these guys to replace the **Dick Payne** (q.v.). But there's just one in the unlisted records, in WI.

Dick Glover: *See also* **Dick Lover**, which is just as bad. Public phone book listings in Saraland, AL; Gardenerville, NV; Aledo, TX and Odessa, TX.

Dick Good: Looking for some GOOD, DICK? Sure you are. Find them in OH, CA, WA, GA, and MN. For variety, Dick Goode (the Dan Quayle version?) can be found in OK, TN, VA, WV, FL and WA.

Dick Goodbody: Well, if you're going to dick somebody, you may as well dick a goodbody. There are a whole passel of them in the unlisted records (as Richard) in CA, KS, NY, and NJ.

Dick Goodcock: While Goodcock does exist as a family name, I could find no Dicks or Richards in either the public or unlisted directories. But I included this information so you wouldn't feel the need to go looking.

Dick Goodfriend: Hey, sometimes in your life it's not only your good friend, it's the only friend you've got. As for dicking a good friend—did you see *When Harry Met Sally*? There are a good number of Dick Goodfriends in the listings (as Richard) in IL, MD, KS, CA, WI and MO.

Dick Goodhead: This fully makes up for the fact that there is no **Dick Goodcock** (q.v.), doesn't it? There are several of them (under Richard) in OR and WA. There are some women listed with this name as well, and I can't help but wonder how they feel about it. Historical note: In the early 1970s, *National Lampoon* used to feature a column detailing the autobiographical adventures of a very social young lady named Cynthia Goodhead.

Dick Gott: Gott Dick? If not, look in CO and TX.

Dick Gozinia: Hard to believe, but there are three guys out there with this name. Found in SC, OH and AZ.

*** MASKED DICK ***

Dick Grayson—Robin (from Batman &Robin).

Dick Greek: Roommate of Ben Dover? I hear these guys are a pain in the ass. There are quite of few of them in the public records (as Richard) in NE, MO, FL, CA, IL, MI, TX, and OH.

Dick Green: See a doctor right away if you get this. Or maybe they're Martians? If so, they're getting ready to invade. Look at all these listings: you can look them up in the public phone books of Canyon Country, CA; Mira Loma, CA; Stockton, CA, Wheat Ridge, CO; Clayton, DE; Viola, DE, Bradenton, FL; Honolulu, HI; Mount Ayr, IA; Preston, IA; Greenup, IL; Savanna, IL; Ludlow, MA, Earleville, MD; Caseville, MI; Andover, MN; Rosemount, MN; Charlotte, NC; Rapid City, SD; Virginia Beach, VA; Ione, WA; Spokane, WA; Fort Dodge, IA; Magnolia, TX; Sylva, NC; Roan Mountain, TN; Mansfield, TX; Many, LA; Steamboat Springs, CO; Carson City, NV; Bethlehem, PA; and Manhattan, KS.

*** CELEBRITY DICK ***

Dick Gregory: (1932–) Comedian, entertainer who became very popular in the early 1970s for his satirical views on American racial issues.

Dick Grinder: Is that the little Italian guy with the monkey and the...um...organ? Or is this how you make **Dick Sparks** fly from **Dick Steele** (q.v.)? There is just one of these guys left, in ID.

*** CELEBRITY DICK ***

Dick Grob: Elvis Presley's bodyguard, author. He first met Elvis in 1967 when he was a Palm Springs, CA police officer. Elvis persuaded Grob to leave his job and become head of Elvis' security organization, a position he held until Elvis' death. Grob later wrote a book, *The Elvis Conspiracy.*

Dick Groh: Must be what happens when you give Viagra to Dick Withers (*see* that listing)...found only in CA, incidentally.

Dick Gunn: Another one of the "cool" names in this list. You wouldn't want to mess with a guy named Dick Gunn. Sounds like a Clint Eastwood character. There's a couple of these guys out there, in MA and KY.

Dick Hail: As it appears in the directories, it reads **Hail, Dick**. Which is appropriate if the Leader is a dick, which he often is. But **Dick Hail** sounds like what they get in Texas and other midwest States occasionally, that leaves lots of dents in the sheet metal of your car. One lucky fella in NY has this name.

Dick Hair: Not everybody has it. Some go to **Dick Barber** or **Dick Shaver** (q.v.). One thing is for sure: you don't want to find one in your food when you go out to eat. If you're looking for dick hair, they're pretty easy to find (as you probably guessed). They can be found (all as Richard) in the public phone books of Dublin, CA; Highland, CA; San Bernardino, CA; Washington, DC; Brandon, FL; Crest Hill, IL; O'Fallon, IL; South Bend, IN; West Monroe, LA; Saginaw, MI; Minot, ND; Wewoka, OK; York, PA; Blythewood, SC; Jamestown, SC; Newport, TN; San Antonio, TX; Cabot, AR; Colorado Springs, CO; Walla Walla, WA; Kansas City, MO; Isle of Palms, SC; St. Helens, OR; Shermans Dale, PA; and with unlisted numbers (as Richard) in CA, WA, CO, AZ, TX, AR, LA, MO, IL, ND, MI, IN, FL, NC, SC, PA, NY and MA.

Dick Hammer: Probably one of the most masculine names in the world. Seriously. I'm considering it as a pseudonym. *"Ladies can't resist.... Dick Hammer!"* A few lucky guys out there have it, in Naples, FL; St. Augustine, FL; Greensboro, NC; Burlington, WA; Sheridan, WY; and Westville, OK.

Dick Hand: They go together.... naturally, don't they? For the majority of guys, the dick hand is the right. Find them in Juneau, AK and Mobridge, SD. For more anatomical funnies, *see,* also, **Dick Foote, Dick Head, Dick Eye,** and **Dick Lung.**

Dick Hard: Yup, there's a man in GA listed under this name.

Dick Harden: Hopefully, yours does. At appropriate times, of course. Quite a few of these gentlemen can be found, yes, as Dick, in IL, OH, IA, MD, NJ and MO, and more, as Richard in CA, AZ, CO, WY, TX, IN, FL, GA, ID, NC, WV, VA, MD, PA, NY, CT, NJ, NH, MA, KY, MS, AL, TN, OH, IA, MI, OK and MO—luckily for you girls.

Dick Harder: When just plain "hard" isn't enough, you can look for this guy in CA.

Dick Hardick: I guess there are worse things you can be called than "hardick." Must be rough as a kid, though. They are out there (as Richard) in CA, MI, OH, MD, NJ,

Dick Hardman: They say a hard man is good to find. Look for them in WA, OK, PA, OH, IL, and GA.

*** CINEMATIC DICK ***

Dick Harper:—One of the title movie characters in *Fun With Dick And Jane* (1977), starring George Segal, Jane Fonda. An upper-middle-class couple turns to robbery to pay their bills. A 2005 remake starring Alec Baldwin, Jim Carrey and Tea Leoni is in the works.

*** CELEBRITY DICK ***

Dick Haymes (1916–1980) Actor, singing star of the 1940s; did movies (e.g. *Four Jills In A Jeep*, 1944) and TV (e.g. *Adam 12*).

Dick Head: Well we certainly know there are a lot of dick heads out there, but who knew they'd be listed in the phone book? Go figure. Dick Head probably goes to **Dick Barber** (q.v.) to trim his **Dick Hair** (q.v.). They can be found in Westford, MA; Granite Falls, NE; New York, New York; as well as in OK, NC, VA, PA, TX, AK, CA, NV, LA, UT, WI, WA, NJ, CO, MO, MT, IN, TN, FL, PA, RI, ID, SC, CT, IL, OH, OR, MN, and WY.

Dick Health: Something we all want. To get it and maintain it, you should *see* **Dick Doctor.** There is just one Dick Health out there (only as Richard) in Indiana.

Dick Healthy: When you come back from the **Dick Doctor** (q.v.) and she asks you how you are, this is what you say. Just one listed out there (as Rick) in TX.

Dick Heart: Well, you've seen the movie *Braveheart*, right? This could be the story of those guys who weren't so noble. There are a bunch of them out there (listed as Richard) in CA, OH, CO, CT, WI, ND, IL and TX.

Dick Herr: Also looks good as HERR, DICK, although it changes the meaning completely. Listed in TX, IN, NY and CA.

Dick Hertz: This painful condition can be found in Polson, MT and Queens, NY phone books (*See also* Dick Hurt and Dick Hurts, if you're so inclined).

Dick Hitler: Sieg hard! I had no idea that anybody still had the name Hitler, especially not outside Germany. According to an article I read in *The New Yorker* back in 2000, Hitler did have relatives who moved to America (in particular, a nephew named Patrick Hitler), but after WWII they all changed their names. And Hitler still has living relatives in Germany—he didn't just get spawned in a test tube, you know—who still keep the name and who insist that their famous ancestor was misunderstood.

As with almost any surname, not everybody who has it is related (except in my case—as it happens, anybody and everybody with my name is related). So the Hitlers I found in the public records search might have no relation whatever to old Adolf. Still, you gotta wonder about anybody named Hitler, and whether they feel that it is a burden, or maybe even a badge of honor, depending on their particular circle of friends. In any event, there are two Richard Hitlers in the records: one in AR, one in MS.

So, you might be wondering: are there any *other* Hitlers in America? Yeah! A bunch! Am I the only one who didn't know this?

Here's what I found:

In the public phone books, you can find:

Adolf Hitler in North Hollywood, CA.
Ron Hitler in Lemon Grove, CA.
C. Hitler in Chicago, IL.
Michael Hitler in Louisville, KY.
George Hitler: two of them, in Chapel Hill, NC and Powell, OH.
Ludwig C. Hitler in Circleville, OH.
Sue and Peter Hitler in Cedarburg, WI.
Peter S. Hitler in Milwaukee, WI.

Now, in the unlisted phone records, you can also find these additional Hitlers:

Anita Hitler in California.
A. Hitler in New York.
Joyce and Andrew Hitler in Maine.
Adolf Hitler, age 87, in NJ; another Adolf in IL, one in TX.
Adolf U. Hitler in Delaware.
Adolf T. Hitler in California.
Appolomi Hitler in New Jersey.
Adolpho Hitler, age 96, in Maine.
Betty Hitler in Indiana.
Brooke Hitler in NJ.
Balasubramanian Hitler in Wisconsin.
Another Brooke Hitler in Michigan.
Bruce Hitler in Missouri. (*Bruce Hitler?!?!?*)
Charlotte Hitler in Massachusetts.
Crisanne L. Hitler in Ohio.
Carrey Hitler in Delaware.
Christine and Christopher Hitler in Missouri.
Chris Hitler in Pennsylvania.
Diana Hitler in Missouri.
Louis and Dorothy Hitler in Missouri.
Eric Hitler in Pennsylvania.
Fritz Hitler in Idaho.
Gene Hitler in Utah.
George Hitler, several of them, in OH, NC, UT, FL and SC.
Martha Hitler in Missouri.
Turney and Verna Hitler in California.
James Hitler in California.
Tamika Hitler in Colorado. (*Tamika Hitler?!?*)
Betty Hitler in Indiana.
Ungar Hitler in Colorado.
Prince Hitler in California. (*What a visual I get with THAT name! Think of Michael Jackson's kid and "The Artist Formerly Known As…"*)
Karen Hitler in Arkansas.
Kathryn Hitler in South Carolina.
Michael Hitler in Pennsylvania.

Selvan Hitler in California.
William Hitler in Massachusetts.

I would imagine that having the name Hitler has got to affect your life. But maybe not. Maybe, like anything else, if you've had it all your life, you don't even think about it. Maybe they even have Jewish friends who laugh about it. Ok, a nervous laugh.

And here's an interesting footnote about names which are horrible in our culture: "Osama" has been, since 2001, the single *most popular name* for newborn babies in the Muslim world.

Dick Ho: Sounds like a phrase from a hip hop song, but it's a name, and not a rare one either. Found in the public records in CA, PA, MO, MA and IL.

Dick Hoar: Some readers might say, "That's cruel, to make fun of somebody's name like that!" Hey, listen up: I'm not making fun of anybody's name. If your name happens to be something like **Dick Hoar** and that's the way you choose to be listed on your public records, and I just happen to point that out in a compilation like this, where's the cruelty? I'm not the one who gave him the name or forced him to use it! Anyway, there's more than one **Dick Hoar** in this country and you can find them in OH, CA and FL.

Dick Hogg: We've all met a few of these in our day. But they can be found—several of them—all in TX.

Dick Holden: If you want to know where somebody is Holden, Dick, look in Hot Springs, AR; Simsbury, CT, Debary, FL and The Villages, FL.

Dick Hole: Among the more awful names you could have, I think. Again, it begs the question: why? Why? People go to court and spend money to get their names changed who have started out with much better names than this. Incredibly, two Dick Holes are out there, with unlisted numbers, in NY and CA. For goodness sakes, don't bother them; they have enough troubles.

Dick Holder: There are several gentlemen with this visually graphic name, including a voice-over talent artist (those are the professionals whose voices are used to narrate TV and radio commercials, etc., where the speaker is not shown), and three or four ordinary dick holders with unlisted numbers in TX, OR and IN.

Dick Holster: The quintessential label for a woman who isn't good for anything else. And a very special name that can be found in public records for a few guys living in WI, PA, TX, NJ and CA. Hey Girls! How would you like to be known as Mrs. Dick Holster?

Dick Homo: This incredible name falls into the same category as **Dick Queer** (q.v.). Two are found out there (as Richard) in NH and FL.

Dick Honey: It takes a very special kind of bee to produce this. As you can imagine, it is extremely rare: public records say just one guy has this name, in OR.

Dick Hood: Presumably not Jewish. **Dick Mechanic** (q.v.) looks under here to see why it won't start. Found in WA, OR, TX, OK, IA, GA, NC, VA, GA, AL, and SC.

Dick Horn: One of the most satisfying musical instruments, and those who can blow it properly are held in very high esteem. Dick Horns can be found in Stateline, NV; Zephyr Cove, NV; McKinney, TX; Spooner, WI; and South Lake Tahoe, CA.

Dick Horni: The surname Horni really exists, and one gentleman of this family had a manufacturing business—The Horni Corp.—that made fire alarm boxes and traffic signals back in the 1930s and 40s. Sorry to say, no Dicks or Richards by this name are found in the public records, but it was worth mentioning.

Dick Horny: I can relate. At least three guys in IN, NY and CA are in the books (as Richard).

Dick Horse: I would love to be able to tell people, "Look me up in the book under Horse, Dick." A few lucky guys in WA, OK, CA and SD can truthfully say that (as Richard). *See,* also, **Dick Moose.**

Dick House: There are a surprising number of Dick Houses out there, but what goes on inside, you'll have to discover for yourself. They can be found in Gassville, AR; San Jose, CA; Arthur, IL; Brookville, KS; Salina, KS; Branson, MO; Helena, MT; Norman, OK; Tichnor, OK; Paris, TX; and Rye, NY.

Dick Huge: If you want to see Huge, Dick, you'll find him in Michigan. I knew that this was one of the first listings you would look for.

Dick Hummer: At least three of these musical fellas have unlisted numbers in CA and NC.

Dick Hung: The jury is out on just how hung he is. Plenty of them out there, in OR, CA and FL.

Dick Hunger: Satisfy this the right way and you may get a full belly. There are a bunch of them out there (all listed as Richard), in OR, CA, IN, ME, MI, MO, WA, PA and FL.

Dick Hunt: Hey, we used to play that game! 15 of these fellas are found in public phone books: Indio CA:, Penryn CA; Snellville, GA; Tallahassee FL; Woodstock GA; Emmett ID; Clinton NC; Trenton NJ: Kearney NE; Schenectady NY; Greenville OH; Dell City TX; Oshkosh WI; and Cave City KY.

Dick Hunter: I guess this is who goes on a Dick Hunt. What kind of camouflage outfit do you wear for this kind of hunting? RealDick? As expected, there are quite a few of these out there, especially during the current man shortage. Listings found in AZ, ID, GA, TX, IL, IA, MS, NC, ME, KS, HI, OK, CA, NV, LA, AR, CO and PA.

Dick Hurt: At least three different men are out there with this unfortunate name, according to the AOL white pages (note: Ophelia Hurt is listed in the Chicago phone book). *See also* Dick Hertz, Dick Hurts.

Dick Hurts: Incredible, that at least six guys are currently going through life with this name. Understandably, their numbers are unlisted. But they live in CA, MD, MI, VA, IA and MA.

Dick Hustler: A gigolo? A gay prostitute? Either way, not an enviable moniker. But there are a few men by this name in VT, MO and WA.

Dick Hyman: A name that has doubtless launched a thousand conversations. One older gentleman in FL is found in the unlisted books with this name (many more as Richard).

Dick Hymen: Mortal enemies paired up as a name, like Snake Mongoose. And yet, one dude in CA (as Richard) is known by this name.

Dick Indyke: There's something you don't see too often, unless she's in the closet or a hooker. They're all in NY and IL (as Richard).

Dick Insert: From the *Geek Sex Manual*, this is "step 219." And it's also the name of a unique fellow in CT (as Richard).

Dick Jack: When yours goes flat, take one of these out of the trunk so you can get it up. There's a whole bunch of Dick Jacks out there, in Anderson, IN; Manteo, SC; Fulshear, TX; Roanoke, VA; Wirtz, VA; and Purcell, OK.

Dick Jackoff: No Dicks with this name turned up in my search. Darn! No Richards, either. However, there are nine people in the records with this last name, and I don't envy them. One of them, by the way, is in the records as Fast M. Jackoff, with an unlisted number. In NY, there are two Richard Jacoffs. Close enough.

Dick Jewel: When earrings and necklaces just aren't enough. Get one fitted in that cock ring. Found in WI and OH.

Dick Justice: When *this* reality show appears on Court TV, I'll watch it. Two guys found in the public phone books of Urbandale, IA and Oliver Springs, TN.

Dick Judge: Who else is going to judge the dick contests? Or hand out **Dick Justice** (q.v.). Four Dick Judges are out there, in Nashville, IN; Ogdensburg, NY; Rochester, NY and Columbus, IN. *See,* also: **Dick Law, Dick Police.**

Dick King: It's good to be the King. Just ask these lucky guys in WA, OR, SC, NC, NY, VA and CA.

Dick Kisser: Another tough name to go through life with. At least three different guys with this name are indicated as unlisted in the AOL white pages.

Dick Klitgaard: Sounds like a women's personal hygiene product, or one worn during sports activities. One (as Richard) lives in Iowa.

Dick Knight: Rides in to save the fair lady from **Dick Dragon** (q.v.). These armored heroes can be found in WA, OR, ID, TX, IL, OH, TN, AL, FL, GA, SC, NC, TN, AZ, UT, IN, MS, KY, CA, NV and LA. There are other jokes you can make with this name, but they're so obvious, I'll let you do it so you can amuse yourself with how clever you are.

Dick Knott: I think I once saw a photo of some African tribesmen who could do this. Here in America you can find them in MO, FL, IL and GA.

Dick Kool: As with **Dick Cool** (*q.v.*), one of the few names in this book I would like to have. Just for a day. And this more popular spelling can be found in NE, GA, CA, MI, OH, SD, GA, WI, MI, FL and MD.

Dick Kunt: Are there really people in this country whose last name is Kunt? Yes, and they are in the unlisted number records. There is a record of an "A. Kunt" in KY; a "U. Kunt" in NY; and several other people with a variety of names, some American-sounding, some foreign sounding. I will leave it to you to do your own research, if you care to do so. I am almost relieved to say that there is no record of either a Dick Kunt nor a Richard Kunt. Life should not be that cruel. However, *see* the next entry.

Dick Kuntz: Two great names that fit like a hand in glove. Listed in the Burlingame, KS phone book (Ophelia Kuntz has several listings in the AOL white pages).

Dick LaCock: It's no joke, they're out there, a handful of them (haha)…all in PA and OR, all listed as Richard.

Dick Lake: It's really only 6 inches deep, but its owners claim it's 10 inches. Found in the public phone directories of Milton, FL and Endicott, NY. *See*, also: **Dick Shore.**

Dick Lamb: This is how March goes out (for the rest of the weather report, *see* **Dick Lion**). At least it does in Antoich, CA; Phoenix, AZ; Yuma, AZ; Green River, WY; Broomfield, CO; Christiana, TX; Mexico, MO; Dalton City, IA; Davenport, IA; St. Peters, MO; Mitchellsburg, KY; Eagleville,

TN; Longboat Key, FL; Keezletown, VA; Washington, DC; and New York, NY. Check The Weather Channel for more details.

Dick Lane: Well, if there's a Fast Lane, and a car pool lane, then why not? Find them in Sulphur Rock, AR; Half Moon Bay, CA; Blanca, CO; West Hartford, CT; Mount Carmel, IL; Plymouth, MA; Benton Harbor, MI; Buchanan, MI; Excelsior, MN; Minneapolis, MN; Ketchum, OK; Tulsa, OK; Vinita, OK; Dyersburg, TN; Plano, TX; and Chaparral, NM.

Dick Land: Great name for a gay night club. But when you find these in the phone book, I doubt very much that's what they are. Men with this name are listed in Phenix City, AL; New Castle, IN; and Kent, WA.

Dick Large: there are at least 6 dudes out there with this name: three in OH, and also in NJ, CA and UT.

Dick Lather: This must be what **Dick Shaver** uses on that **Dick Stubble** (q.v.). You could find these guys in CO, FL, OH, AK, PA, and WA (as Richard) if they didn't have unlisted numbers.

Dick Law: Heavy penalties for violating the Dick Law. Just ask any woman. And when you violate the Dick Law, you get arrested by the **Dick Copp** (q.v.). These guys are living in CA, UT, IL, MI, NV, CO, CA, AZ and MO.

Dick Lawless: Of course, wherever Dick Law rules, you are going to find…the Dick Lawless. It's just how life is. These Lawless, Dicks can be found in the public phone directories of Penn Valley, CA and Commercial Point, OH.

Dick Lawyer: Is this the guy who screws **Dick Client** (q.v.)? Several listings found, all in Indiana.

Dick Leak: The guy who invented *Depends*? If so, which one? There are several (as Richard) in NC, SC, GA, KS, NJ, FL, CA and IL.

*** ANTHROPOLOGICAL DICK ***

Dick Leakey: (1944–) World-renowned paleo-anthropologist.

Dick Leakey: What a Chinaman with gonorrhea says to his doctor? Ask this one guy who lives in Indiana with an unlisted number.

Dick Leisure: Aaahhh, just lying there in a chaise lounge, sucking on a St. Pauli Girl. Or vice versa. Found in AR, and also (as Richard) in AZ, TX, MD, IN, AL, FL and OH.

Dick Less: A failed sex-change? A circumcision gone awry? A Ken doll? Only in CA, but he's there.

Dick Lesser: Even sadder, if that's possible…just one listed in UT.

Dick Lick: Has an unlisted number in New York.

Dick Licker: This is a name you wouldn't think is really out there, yet there are at least three different listings in AOL white pages, plus three more as "Richard."

Dick Light. Tastes great. Less filling. Get a taste in Salinas, CA and Lancaster, SC.

Dick Link: For those who prefer this kind over **Dick Bacon** (q.v.). You can find these in ID, CO, OK, IL, IA, WI, MN, and IL.

Dick Lipps: Multiples of them can be found in AOL white pages as unlisted.

Dick Little: LITTLE, DICKs can be found in Peoria, AZ; Pleasant Plains, IL; Las Vegas, NV; Pembine, WI; Macon, GA; Chattanooga, TN; Newville, PA; Simi Valley, CA; and also unlisted in FL, IN, MI, WI, MS, WA, IL, TX, GA; there is also a Dickens Little in NY. I'm sure you girls have had your share of LITTLE, DICKs, haven't you? And let's not forget comedian/impressionist Rich Little, who, after all, is a Richard, which makes him a Dick Little when you really get down to it.

Dick Littleboy: Michael Jackson's alter ego? According to the unlisted phone records, one resides in NY, the other in OR.

Dick Littlecock: A tough, tough name to go through life with. The public records database shows just one person with this surname, and it's a woman. However, she has to have a father by the same name, wouldn't you think? But I can't find him. Maybe she can't either. A name like this could make somebody want to disappear. There are no Dicks or Richards in the records with this surname, but they might be out there. Hiding.

Dick Lion: March comes in like Dick Lion, and goes out like **Dick Lamb**. At least in TX, where this one is listed (as Richard). (*See also* Dick Lyon).

Dick Lively: According to the records, there is a LIVELY, DICK in OR. Control yourselves, ladies.

*** LITERARY DICK ***

Dick Locher: (1929–) Pulitzer Prize winning editorial cartoonist at the Chicago Tribune and artist of the **Dick Tracy** (q.v.) comic after 1983.

Dick Locke: You don't want to be caught in one of these. Firemen might have to come get you out with the Jaws of Life. So be very careful in OR, CA, WY, MI, OH, FL, NE, MI, SC and VT.

Dick Long: This was one of the first names you looked for, wasn't it? You are just sooooo predictable. There are 11 of them found in public phone books, listed as LONG, DICK: in Heber, AZ; Milford, IA; Cumberland MD; Presque Isle, ME; Middletown, VA; Mount Sterling, OH; and Dublin, PA.

Dick Longing: The pangs of a deprived woman. And of one guy in Arkansas.

Dick Longstreet: Not a particularly hysterical name, but worth a chuckle. There are so many out there I won't bother to list the 16 States in which they are found (all as Richard).

Dick Lovely: It's nice to know that there are a couple of LOVELY, DICKs out there: one in LaFollette, TN; one in Kissimmee, FL. Yes, there's a Lovely, Dick in Kissimmee, you fool.

Dick Lover: Great name for a female porn star (or gay one, I suppose) but could cause problems otherwise. Nonetheless, the AOL white pages say there are several of these fellas with unlisted numbers.

Dick Loving: Now, if you're going to be a guy, and have this name, you'd darn well better be gay, or else life is just going to be unbearable. Of course there's another way to read the name, as in, "Hey baby, gimme some Dick Loving." Or a woman could say that to the guy with this name. But you have to know that anybody with this name is so sick of hearing the jokes, they carry a gun. I don't know if the men with this name are gay or not, or if they carry guns, but there are at least three of them and they all live in VA.

Dick Loser: Probably the saddest name in this book. Two guys, one in OH and one in TX, actually go through life with these names.

Dick Lucky: Now there's somebody to envy. Two Lucky Dicks are out there: one in CA, one in LA.

Dick Lumber: What guy wouldn't want a piece of lumber in his shorts? Timmmmmmmmberrrrrrrr, ladies! There's one in the unlisted books (as Richard) in NJ.

Dick Lump: Is it a tumor? Or just a cyst? You'd be a fool to delay seeing **Dick Doctor** (q.v.). Dick Lumps can be found (only as Richard) in MI, CA, TX, FL, and NY.

Dick Lung: A rare medical condition, caused by too much Dick Smoking? One guy in San Francisco, CA has this moniker.

Dick Lust: It's not just a great concept, it's…a person! Quite a few of them, in fact, in the unlisted number records (as Richard) in CA, WI, OH, DE, OK, TX, MN, FL, NH and NY.

Dick Lustgarden: A lust garden? What are they planting there? Maybe we should ask **Dick Farmer** or **Dick Gardener** (q.v.). Just one out there (as Richard) in PA.

Dick Lyon: Listed as LYON, DICK: Found in CA, AZ, IL, MN, WI, MI, NY, OK, and MA. We've all known some lyon dicks in our day. *See also* **Dick Lion**. I am Dick, hear me roar!

Dick Major: An apt description of a lot of college girls. At least, the ones you want to meet. Also, the names of two guys in MI and MO. *See,* also: **Dick Minor.**

*** CELEBRITY DICK ***

Dick Martin: (1922–) Co-star of groundbreaking TV series *Rowan & Martin's Laugh-In.* Director of many popular TV shows, including *The Bob Newhart Show; Mama's Family; Newhart; Family Ties; The Redd Foxx Show;* and *In The Heat Of The Night.*

Dick Mason: You get one of these guys, and a **Dick Carpenter,** and a **Dick Plummer** (q.v.), and you can build yourself a **Dick House** (q.v.). These fellas are found in CA, NM, AZ, TX, CO and OR.

Dick Master: Is this a very special exercise machine? Or the natural mate for **Dick Slave** (q.v.)? The answer lies with one man in Ohio.

Dick Maus: Can't you just picture him nibbling on **Dick Cheese?** For more of these puerile jokes, *see* the entries for **Dick Mouse** and **Dick Katz.** One guy with this name lives in California.

Dick Measure: According to all the reference books, six inches is the average. For anything much beyond that, demand proof. Most guys put the ruler away and stop checking by the time they turn 20. However, for a very select group out there, it's a lifetime name. Just one found, in New Jersey.

Dick Mechanic: This is a man who every guy needs to have on speed dial. If yours doesn't work, he'll put it up on the lift, check under the hood, and see what's wrong. Maybe you just need a new hose. Or a belt. These guys are out there (listed as Richard) in WI, FL, NC, WA, and WI.

Dick Meet: The kind of competition that you train for all year. There's one in the records (a Richard) in Oregon.

Dick Mercury: You look sick. He needs to take your temperature. Do you prefer oral or rectal? Rectal is more accurate, you know. Catch the fever…in MO, OH, NY and FL.

Dick Messing: The aftermath of a **Dick Storm** (q.v.)? One listing, in TX.

Dick Milk: You can't make up stuff like this. However, in the interests of this book's integrity as well as my own, I must state that the listing says "Richard," not "Dick." Still…. we can call him Dick Milk. There's one listed in Austin, TX; and several unlisted ones in NY, OH, GA, FL and MA. Got Dick Milk? This book does! See, also: **Dick Cream** and **Dick Cheese**, in the dairy section.

Dick Minor: Don't do this, because as the old saying goes, "15 will get you 20." Good advice for Michael Jackson. A bunch of different guys by this name can be found in CO, NE, IL, IA, NC and MI.

Dick Mo: Mo, Dick: what the inner-city woman demands? Must be, because there are a bunch of them (as Richard) in CA, CO, NY, PA, NH, TX, MN, VA, ME, and MA.

Dick Money: I've heard of hard cash, but this is a new one on me. What's the motto: "E Pluribus Ummmmmmmmmmmm"? One guy in FL knows whose portrait is printed on this currency.

Dick Monster: The only thing that could be better would be if his middle name was "one eyed purple headed." Is this the one that ate San Francisco? One Richard Monster has an unlisted number in CA.

Dick Moore: Need Moore, Dick? You can find listings for them in CA, WA, NM, UT, CO, TX, OK, AR, NE, KS, MO, IL, MT, NE, WI, IA, MI, IN, OH, TN, AL, FL, GA, SC, NC, VA, PA, NY, ME. There's MOORE, DICK practically everywhere you look!

*** CELEBRITY DICK ***

Dickie Moore (1925–) Actor; one of the original Little Rascals.

Dick Moorhead: Another great name for a porno star. You can find one in the Belton, TX phone book. And there's a Dick Moorehead in PA.

Dick Moose: Bet you didn't think you could find Moose, Dick in the phone books, did you? One proud man in OH claims this title (as well as so many Richards there isn't room to list them). *See* also **Dick Horse.**

Dick Moron: Stop it, you're saying. "Moron" cannot be a real family name. Can it? According to the public records database, it is. And four men out there, in four different States—AL, MN, TX and TN—bravely go through life with the name Richard Moron. If you're low enough to laugh at that, be my guest. And while you're at it, *see* **Dick Genius.**

*** POLITICAL DICK ***

Dick Morris: Prominent American political consultant; advisor to former President Bill Clinton for over 20 years. Author, *Off With Their Heads: Traitors, Crooks & Obstructionists in American Politics, Media & Business.*

Dick Moss: Any relation to **Dick Forest** or **Dick Shaver** (q.v.)? You'll have to ask them. If you've got dick moss, maybe you need to pay more attention to your personal hygiene. These guys are in Glendale, CA; Tahoma, CA; Newberry, FL; Daytona Beach, FL; and Peru, IN.

Dick Mouse: Is that a rodent in your pants, or are you just happy to see me? Four examples out there, all in AK and VA (all Richards). There are also a *lot* of listings for **Dick Katz,** which is not a funny name in and of itself, except when juxtaposed with **Dick Mouse,** as I've done here. What would be funny, though, is if somehow a **Dick Katz** got into a fight with a **Dick Mouse** and started chasing him. You think about that. And *see* the entry for **Dick Maus.**

Dick Munch: Found the little rascal, only in AR.

Dick Muscle: For many guys, the only one that ever gets any exercise. Work out! One guy in New Jersey (as Richard) has this name in the unlisted records.

Dick Nazi: Well, you *have* to be a dick to be a Nazi, but are there really people out there with the family name Nazi? Yes. Judging by many of the first names of folks in the directories with this surname, it appears to be of Middle Eastern origin. Perhaps the Dick Nazi, in the style of the Soup Nazi, expresses his displeasure by shouting, *'No dick for you!"* In any event, the AOL white pages indicate at least three Dick Nazis out there, perhaps waiting for their Reich, or something, to rise again.

Dick Neck: Considering some of the names in this book, you'd think there would be one of these, wouldn't you? But despite a diligent search, I found no Dick Neck, nor even a Richard Neck, in the public records. There was a "D. Neck;" that *might* be a Dick. Why else would he list himself only as "D."? Anyway, if that *is* a Dick Neck, he belongs directly below **Dick Head** (q.v.).

Dick Needle: When I searched for NEEDLE, DICK, I really wasn't expecting to find any; fortunately for this book, I found two: West Palm Beach, FL and an unlisted one in GA. What can I say?

Dick Needy: There are two NEEDY, DICKs with unlisted numbers out there, both in Indiana. Please give till it hurts.

Dick Nibbler: Sounds like a girl we'd all like to meet. Yes, there are two in the directories: one in OR, one in MN.

Dick Nigger: There is no Dick Nigger in the public records. But I found, to my horror, that there is a David Nigger and Erin Nigger in Georgia; a Robert Nigger in MD; a Bob K. Nigger in FL; a Billy J. Nigger in Ohio; a Tashika Nigger in New York; and a Karnail Nigger in New Jersey. All have unlisted numbers, and we need not ask why.

Dick Nipple: Pacifier from an adult novelty store? There's a guy with this name in the public phone book in Argyle, WI.

*** BIGGEST DICK OF ALL TIME ***

Dick Nixon: (1913–1994) Thirty-seventh President of the United States. He had been Vice President under Dwight Eisenhower for two terms from

1952–1960, then lost the race for President against John F. Kennedy by a razor-thin margin in 1960.

He was elected to two terms in 1968 and 1972 as a Republican, but resigned on 8 August 1974 to avoid what appeared to be an imminent threat of impeachment. Known popularly as "Tricky Dick," especially after Congress' investigation into the break-in at Democratic Party headquarters in the Watergate Hotel (17 June 1972) uncovered a "dirty tricks" operation in Nixon's Committee To Re-Elect The President (CREEP).

Nixon's running mate and Vice President was former Maryland governor Spiro T. Agnew. Always unpopular with the press, whom he often traded droll barbs with (he called them, among other things, "nattering nabobs of negativism"), Agnew got caught up in a separate scandal of his own, arising out of tax irregularities while he was Governor. He resigned as Vice President in 1973 after pleading "no contest" to tax evasion charges. Around the same time, several top Nixon aides had been fired and/or indicted in connection with the Watergate break-in. The sharks were circling; blood was in the water.

During the Watergate hearings in Congress, it was discovered that Nixon secretly tape-recorded many conversations which took place in the Oval Office. After a court battle, the heavily edited tapes which Nixon turned over strongly suggested that although he had no prior knowledge of the break-in, he participated in discussions about sidetracking the investigation: that would form the basis for a charge of obstruction of justice.

There was much public debate about whether what Nixon did constituted "high crimes and misdemeanors," which is the Constitutional standard for impeaching a President. But impeachment is an accusation; the question of whether enough evidence existed for a conviction (and removal from office) would be resolved at a trial. Nixon apparently did not want to suffer the indignity of an impeachment, or else he feared the evidence would be sufficient for conviction and he did not want to leave office under those circumstances. By resigning—the only President to ever do so—Nixon technically left office with a "clean record."

Nixon made bold strides in foreign policy, opening relations with China by visiting in 1972 and reducing tensions with the Soviet Union somewhat by visiting Moscow, but he seemed unable to cope with the cultural upheaval fed by protests over the Vietnam War (which he inherited from President Johnson), Woodstock, drugs, and the coming of age of the restless Baby Boomers. Although he made a couple of attempts to be "cool" (including a cameo on *Rowan And Martin's Laugh-In* in which he said "Sock It To Me!"), his stiffness and paranoid tendencies made him back into a corner over the Watergate scandal rather than cooly glide through it, as Bill Clinton did with the Monica Lewinsky scandal.

As comedian Jackie Mason aptly put it, in comparing Nixon with Clinton, "Bill Clinton is the biggest liar of all time. Nixon was a liar, too, but at least he had the decency to twitch a little bit, because his conscience was bothering him. Clinton has no conscience. He'll tell you a lie. You don't like that one? He's got another lie for you."

After resigning in disgrace, Nixon stayed out of the limelight for several years, then slowly began to rehabilitate himself as a statesman and advisor to Presidents until he died of a stroke in 1994.

Though reviled during his time in office by the hippie generation, in retrospect Nixon was not so much a bad President as he was bad at public relations. Had he handled Watergate with more aplomb, he would probably have finished his second term in office.

Huh? What's that you said? Did you say, "Larry, why are you sticking this crap in your book? This ain't funny!" To you, I say: don't be a dick. Stuff like this adds class and redeeming social value to this otherwise puerile book.

Dick No: Just say NO to Dick, and…. I guess he'll respond, "Yes….?" I know that I would not want to be listed in the phone book as **No Dick.** But there are several out there (as Richard) in OR, TN, CA and IL.

Dick Noose: Rumored to be well hung. Two unlisted gentlemen with this name are in IL and OH.

Dick Nose: Some people are born with handicaps. Others are given them by their parents. This is a real person with a listing in CA.

Dick Nuckles: You don't want to get hit with a fistful of these, that's for sure. Fortunately there's only one of them, in the unlisted records of AR.

Dick Nurse: Every man would love to have a button to press by his bedside to summon one of these. However, they probably would not like it if a real Dick Nurse showed up, like one of the three guys with this name in the State of Washington.

Dick Nutt: Highly prized for their nectar. This rare delicacy is grown only in Jonesboro, AR.

Dick Odor: If you're looking for one of these guys, you might want to hire **Dick Nose** (q.v.). Or, check the public phone directories of Kansas City, MO and Marshalltown, IA (as Richard).

Dick Officer: You might use this in a sentence, e.g., "I wasn't doing dick, Officer;" but then you might wind up with a much *harsher* sentence. A number of Richard Officers are in the books out there (no Dicks), in TX, TN, FL, AZ, CA, MA, TX and NH.

Dick Oil: Very important to use regularly so your crank doesn't get rusty. Found (as Richard) in TX, KS, WI and LA.

Dick Oral: That's the way, *uh-huh uh-huh*, I like it, *uh-huh uh-huh*. A handful of these dudes are located (as Richard) in NY, CA, VA, FL, IL. Now that you know there's a Dick Oral…is there a **Dick Anal**? Go to that part of the book and see for yourself!

Dick Osgood: That's what I like to hear from a lady with a foreign accent! At least three guys in MN are listed with this name.

Dick Outhouse: Most of these have probably been replaced with indoor plumbing. Still, I found one in Creston, IA.

Dick Painter: Wonder if he uses a brush or a roller? If you're looking for a dick painter, they're listed in TX, FL, VA, WI, WV and AZ. And by the way I recommended using a flat finish: doesn't show fingerprints as much as the high gloss.

Dick Paper: I'm not sure if this is a good name for a news tabloid. Four gentlemen with this name have unlisted numbers in NY, OH, CA and MN.

Dick Parker: Sometimes when a woman is too busy, this is what you have to be. If the woman is fancy enough, perhaps she will have a **Dick Valet** (q.v.). Dick Parkers can be found in the public phone listings in Anchorage, AK; Tuscaloosa, AL; Green Valley, AZ; Groveland, CA; Denver, CO; Zephyrhills, FL; Decautur, GA; Fruitvale, ID; Morris, IL: Columbia City, IN; Upland, IN; Kansas City, KS; Sulphur, LA; Princeton, ME; Mansfield, OH; Smithfield, NC; Wooster, OH; Central Point, OR; Amarillo, TX; Buffalo Gap, TX; Arlington, TX; Dallas, TX; Deanville, TX; Houston, TX; Lampasas, TX; Tenaha, TX; Blacksburg, VA; Chesapeake, MD; Pearisburg, VA; Lander, WY; and Dodge City, KS.

Dick Party: Dress casual. Very casual. And be careful about who's throwing it. There is one Dick Party going on out there with an unlisted number (as Richard) in RI.

Dick Payne: Could be the result of venereal disease. Or the result of a **Dick Pierce** (q.v.). Or, could be made of **Dick Glass** and gets replaced by a **Dick Glazier** (q.v.). Found in Napa, CA; Vallejo, CA; Anderson, MO; Camdenton, MO; St. Ann, MO; Warrenton, OR; Yankton, SD (!); DeKalb, TX; and Monroe, UT (an empathetic soul mate, Ophelia Payne, can be found in the public phone books of Olive Branch, MS; Memphis, TN; and Lexington, VA).

Dick Peace: Discover the inner happiness that comes with Dick Peace. Check the public phone directory of Colorado Springs, CO.

Dick Pecker: No Dicks, but there are several Richards in CT…poor sons of bitches.

Dick Pepper: Found next to the **Dick Salt** (q.v.) on the dining room table. The real thing lives in Jackson, MS.

Dick Picker: How do you know when they're ripe? Ask this one guy found in CA.

Dick Pickle: Considering some of the other names in this book, you'd think I'd have found one, but alas, none appear in the public records. *However*, you might be interested to know that there are there guys named **Dill Pickle** out there, and they live in MS, GA and AL.

Dick Pierce: Ouch, ouch, ouch, ouch, ouch, ouch. If you're looking for a dick pierce, I urge you: don't. Try talking to a counselor first and explore why you need to give yourself **Dick Payne** (q.v.). Gentlemen with this name are in the public phone books of Waldron, AR; Ducor, CA; P.C. Beach, FL; Barre, MA; Bristol, ME; Dillon, MT; Lubbock, TX; Spokane, WA; and Cottonwood, CA.

Dick Pigg: That's something that most single guys have done at one point or another, especially when it gets to be about 3:00 AM in the bar and you haven't hooked up with anybody else yet. There is one Dick Pigg in South Carolina, and many, many Richard Piggs in CA, TX, CO, MO, IL, IN, KY, MS, TN, NC, SC, AZ, PA, VA, TN, OR, and FL.

Dick Pink: Imagine opening up a phone book and seeing Pink, Dick. Well, you'll have to imagine it, because all the Dick Pinks out there are in the unlisted records as Richard. They are in NY, TX, NV, NM, MI, CA, MN, IL and GA. And while we're on the subject: is there really a Floyd Pink out there? Yes! Three guys named **Floyd Pink** are in public phone directories as **Pink, Floyd**: in Fort Lauderdale, FL; Punta Gorda, FL; and Dubuque, IA. But wait, it gets even better: *see* **Dick Floyd.**

Dick Plant: Is this what is grown by **Dick Farmer** (q.v.)? And/or by **Dick Gardener** (q.v.)? And is his arch-enemy the notorious **Dick Weed** (q.v.)? Just one found in the public phone listings, appropriately in Gardner, MA.

Dick Player: Only Richards are officially listed, but we know they're all Dick Players. They're found in AZ, TZ, IA, AL, NC, SC, MD, NJ, GA, WA, UT, LA, MS, GA, FL, CA, and NE. Chances are, there's a Dick Player near you! Maybe even in the mirror!

Dick Plucker: I prefer a razor, personally. But at least one guy in SD has this name.

Dick Plummer: Urologists? Found in Grand Rapids, MI; Savage, MN; and Lopez Island, WA.

Dick Poach: Poaching means illegal hunting, and Dick Poachers can be found (as Richard) in CT, OH, VT, NH, NJ, and CO.

Dick Poker: Kind of redundant, if you think about it. Two guys with this name are in the unlisted directories (as Richard) in MA and NY.

*** CELEBRITY DICK ***

Dick Pole: (1950–) Major league baseball player and right-handed pitcher, 1973–1978. Started with the Red Sox, for whom he pitched in the 1975 World Series, and finished major league play with the Mariners. Best year ERA: 4.20. Currently a bench coach with the Cubs.

Dick Police: Do they check you for concealed weapons and suspicious bulges? One fella by this name resides in NJ with an unlisted number. *See,* also: **Dick Law.**

Dick Polisher: In our high-tech age, skilled artisans like this are getting harder and harder to find. But there's a job they probably can't outsource to India! You'll have to go to IL to find one.

Dick Pork: A delicacy that comes from **Dick Pigg** (q.v.)? If you like pork dick, look up this one guy in Texas (under Richard).

Dick Pound: That must be where they take all those stray dicks prowling the streets. Of course, in the listings it looks like Pound, Dick, which is something else entirely. As you well know. If you're looking for the Dick Pound (or Pound, Dick), check the phone directories of Yuma, AZ; and Jefferson, IA.

*** HOLLYWOOD DICK ***

Dick Powell: (1904–1963) Actor; many films (e.g. *The Bad And The Beautiful* [1952]) and TV (e.g., *The Dick Powell Show* (1961–1963).

Dick Power: Let's face it, without power, it doesn't operate. How do you get Dick Power? Use a **Dick Charger** (q.v.). Dick Power is out there, several of them, with unlisted numbers in LA, TX, and PA.

Dick Price: Come on, you've wondered what it's worth! How about women who get sex change operations? They have to buy one. How much? Inquiring minds want to know. Sell it on ebay! These guys can be found in the public phone books of San Francisco, CA (no surprise there); Naples, FL; Ocala, FL; Orange Park, FL; Montezuma, GA; Clear Lake, IA; Bel Air, MD; Roseville, MI; Kansas City, MO; Sunrise Beach, MO; York, NE; Wharton, OH; Prairie City, SD; Burlington, WA; Shelton, WA; Long Pond, PA; Fairfield, IL (plus a "Dicky Price" worth mentioning in La Grange, NC). And after you've checked with Dick Price, you can bargain with **Dick Sales** (q.v.).

Dick Pride: Something we should all have. They have it in MN, AL and NV. Wave it proudly! However, *see* **Dick Shame.**

Dick Proud: Just the adjective form of **Dick Pride,** I guess. There are Proud, Dicks in GA and WA.

Dick Queer: Another one of those names that just makes you wonder, how can someone go through life like that? And yet, there's a chance that if you were to ask one of these guys (there are at least four of them, in OH, PA, NY and WV) that question, they would look at you, puzzled, and say, "What do you mean?" It's like that Monty Python routine where the man's last name is Smoketoomuch. He introduces himself to someone, who laughs and says, "Well, you'd better cut down a little then." Mr. Smoketoomuch doesn't get the joke and it has to be explained to him.

Dick Quick: Sometimes, you just can't wait. Listed in the public phone book of Otsego, MI; also: Dickie Quick, Hopkinsville, KY. But if you have the time, *see* **Dick Slow.**

Dick Rape: Few fathers would be pleased to know their daughter was going out with a guy with this name. And yet, four guys in MS, GA, SC and NJ (as Richard) have presumably, at one time or another, had to sit on the couch with Muffy's dad and make conversation while waiting for her to finish dressing.

Dick Rash: Found only in AZ and CA, thank goodness.

Dick Raw: The main ingredient in that gourmet dish, **Dick Tartar** (q.v.)? Warning: consuming uncooked or undercooked meats may present a high risk of salmonella and other food-borne pathogens. But if you still want to take a chance on raw dick, search the unlisted number records in OR, FL, CA and CO (under Richard).

Dick Razor: This is what **Dick Shaver** uses to remove that **Dick Stubble** after applying a generous amount of hot **Dick Lather** (q.v.). Found in the unlisted records of CA, OH, AR, WA, NC and TX.

Dickson Reardon: Even better than **Dick Reardon**, for which I found no listings. There are two of these guys, in NY and NJ.

*** CELEBRITY DICK ***

Dick Rich: (1909–1967) Actor. Appeared, primarily in supporting or minor roles, in many dozens of films and TV shows, primarily Westerns (*Gunsmoke, Have Gun Will Travel, The Rifleman*, etc.).

Dick Ride: Have you ridden the Dick Ride? I'll bet you have! It goes up and down, up and down, for a few minutes, and after you get off you need a cigarette. Remember, you gotta be "this tall" to go on the Dick Ride. Only "Richards" could be found in my search. They're all in WA, AZ and OH.

Dick Rifle: Long, hard, and can shoot a load a long distance. If you're lucky, you get a *repeating* rifle. But remember, even a muzzle-loader is ready again in 30 seconds if handled by someone with experience. Two interesting gentleman by this name have unlisted numbers in PA and WA.

Dick Ripa: Ouch. Even more frightening than Jack The Ripper. Several (as Richard) found in WV and MD.

Dick Rising: Status report during a romantic evening? Public records show two men by this name, in WA and PA.

Dick Rivers: Is the water yellow? One guy in the public directories has this name, in Safety Harbor, FL.

Dick Roach: Well, girls, if you date a guy named Roach, then Roach, Dick is what you're going to get. And it isn't hard to find roach dick: they're in CA, LA, MI, KY, AL, GA, SC, VA, NY, TX, FL, and IA.

Dick Roads: This is where you'll find **Dick Carr, Dick Buss** and **Dick Trucks,** probably in the **Dick Lane.** Dick roads go through WA, OH, IL, GA, PA and VA.

Dick Roast: Same thing as a wiener roast? Except with real wieners? Ewwwww. Real people with this name live in CA, ME and OR (as Richard).

Dick Rock: I thought I knew music, but this genre seems to have slipped under the radar. UT, FL and KY are home to a few rock dicks.

Dick Rose: When **Dick Doctor** (q.v.) asks you whether the Viagra worked, this is your response. Or could this be one of the varieties raised by **Dick Gardener** (q.v.)? Dick Rose can be found in public phone books in Yreka, CA; Hudson, FL; Longwood, FL; Parma, ID; DeKalb, IL; Fortville, IN; Melrose, MA; Lutsen, MN; Riverside, MO; Wise River, MT; Raleigh, NC; Powell, OH; Bremo Bluff, VA; Riverton, WY; Salem, IN; Columbus, GA; Holly Ridge, NC; Smithfield, NC; and Marysville, CA.

Dick Rubb: And who couldn't use one of these at the end of a long hard day? You can get one (as Richard) in CA, AK, GA, NV, NE, OH and AZ.

Dick Rubba: And who better to give a **Dick Rubb** (q.v.) than someone named Dick Rubba? There are at least one, possibly two, in Michigan.

Dick Ruff: The texture gives extra pleasure to the ladies. There are at least four guys with this name in CA, TX, WI and CO.

Dick Rumplick: Sounds like a real salad-tosser. One found, as Richard, in New York.

*** CELEBRITY DICK ***

Dick Rutan: Pilot of the first non-stop, non-refueled flight around the world, in the lighweight aircraft *Voyager*, in December 1986.

Dick Sales: Just in case you're ever in the market for one, it's good to know that you can shop for them in CA, ME and FL. But before you buy, you might want to check with **Dick Price** (q.v.).

Dick Salt: Can any gourmet kitchen spice rack be complete without this eclectic condiment? Found (as Richard) in better groceries in UT, IL, MI, NY, FL, AZ and WA. And if you're on a low-sodium diet, try *I Can't Believe It's Not Dick Salt*. Also, *see* our other flavors: **Dick Sweet** and **Dick Sour**.

Dick Salter: I guess it's just a matter of taste, like with pretzels. These guys can be found listed in Pace, FL; and unlisted in NV, CO, NY, TX, NC, and AL.

Dick Sand: What you find all over **Dick Beach** (q.v.). And in the unlisted phone records in MN, NM and OH.

Dick Sapp: Not much to say about this one, except that it falls into the same category as **Dick Milk, Dick Cream, Dick Seaman,** and several other entries. If you're looking to collect Dick Sapp, check the phone books in Mesa, AZ; Raiford, FL; Augusta, GA; Chatham, IL; Princeton, IL; Springfield, IL; Phoenix, AZ and Rockford, OH.

*** CELEBRITY DICK ***

Dick Sargent: (1930–1994) Actor. Best known as the second actor to play the role of Darrin Stephens opposite Elizabeth Montgomery on the TV sitcom *Bewitched* from 1969–1972, replacing **Dick York** (q.v.). Dick Sargent sure sounds like a soldier in the **Dick Armey** (q.v.), but isn't.

Dick Sari: In one of Richard Pryor's routines, he talks about how black women are tougher critics of a man's sexual prowess than white women are, and he does an impression of an unsatisfied black woman saying, *"Nigga, that's* *some sorry dick!"* Well, I don't know what's worse: being told you have a sorry dick, or being named Dick Sari. Ask the men listed in the public records by this name (as Richard) in OH, NC, and PA.

Dick Sauer: Being a "SAUER, DICK" can't help when you're looking to get some cranium from a lady (see the entry for **Dick Cranium**). Just ask these guys in Monticello, FL, Sedona, AZ; Norman, OK; Apple Valley, MN; Coeburn, VA and Fort Wayne, IN.

Dick School: If you want to be a happy man, hook up with one of the students here, or better yet: a graduate. Better than that: a graduate *cum laude*. Classes being held now in IL, WI, CA, UT, FL, CT, AZ, and MO (under Richard). Instructors wanted!

Dick Screws: I'll bet he does. There is a whole page of these fellas (all as Richard) in the FL and GA unlisted records.

Dick Seamen: The trouble with this name is that it lacks the subtlety of some of the others. What more can one say about a name like this? At least three of them are noted as unlisted in the AOL white pages—if they aren't stuck together.

Dick Self: You have to be very well hung and/or double jointed to do this, I would imagine. And yet, this is one of most popular suggestions ever made. Three gentlemen in TX, OK and NE have this singular name.

Dick Sellers: Capitalism at its best. You can find one near you in WA, OR, TX, AZ, FL, GA, OK, KS and OH. Or check your Yellow Pages.

Dick Sex: I never would have imagined that "Sex" is a family name, but lo and behold, according to the public records, there are folks out there with this name. It would be fun to see them on Family Feud: the Sex Family! And there are at least six Dick Sexes (listed as Richard) in OH, IL, NY, AR, IN and OH.

Dick Seymour: Wanna SEYMOUR, DICK? Look in the public phone books of Wickenburg, AZ; Palm Desert, CA; Perry, GA; Butte, MT, Amarillo, TX; and LaGrange, WY.

*** CELEBRITY DICK ***

Dick Schaap: (1934–2001) Sports commentator. Won three Emmys for his work on ESPN and three more Emmys for features on ABC's *20/20* and *World News Tonight*.

Dick Schmuck: A little cultural lesson is called for here. In German, "schmuck" means "jewel." However, in Yiddish—the street language of European Jews which they brought with them to America, "schmuck" means "penis." And, as popularly used, it is an insult which is the direct equivalent of calling someone a "dick." It is used when you want to say, "Idiot! Fool! You dope!" On the East and West coasts, *everybody* knows what "schmuck" means. However, in the "Red States," it is possible that this colloquial meaning is not understood.

In New York, there is a famous old story about Judge Schmuck, who presided over Supreme Court in Brooklyn maybe forty or fifty years ago. He used to routinely deny petitions for name changes, and would say to the petitioner, "If I can live with my name, you can live with yours."

For those people out there with the surname Schmuck, it's just something they have to deal with. Especially from idiots like some of the ones reading this book and giggling. But the idea that there are people out there named Dick Schmuck is just one of those strange-but-true facts that makes for humor for people—this author included—whose standards are comparatively low.

Dick Schmucks (all of whom are listed as "Richard") can be found in OR, CA, MO, OK, ND, SD, IL, and OH. Not surprisingly, none are found in NY, NJ, CT or FL. If any had existed there, they got their names changed.

Dick Schmutz: The word "schmutz" (rhymes with "foots") is another Yiddish/German word which has been incorporated into the common lingo of metropolitan East and West Coast venues. "Schmutz" means "dirt," but with a connotation of a stain of unknown origin. As in, "You've got some schmutz on your jacket, you must have leaned against something." There are a few

Dicks named Schmutz in the unlisted records (as Richard) located in UT, FL, KS, IL, NV and NJ.

Dick Schott: Call 911; this is a real emergency. Could **Dick Gunn** (q.v.) be the prime suspect? There are listings for this name in WY, CO, IA, and CA.

*** EXPLORER DICK ***

Francis "Dick" Scobee: (1939–1986) Astronaut who died in Challenger disaster, January 1986.

Dick Shade: Good for cutting down on the glare. Found only in NV and OH.

Dick Shady: Another white rapper? A white, rapping porn actor? I don't know, but I wouldn't buy any used condoms from this guy in ID.

Dick Shaker: At least 3 are found in the AOL white pages with unlisted numbers, and Richard Shakers...who can't fool us, we know they're Dick Shakers...can be found in FL, MA, CT, OH, NY, WI, MN, IA and MD. Whole lotta shakin' goin' on! (Little Richard sang that...another Dick!). Hey wait a minute...we're *all* Dick Shakers at one point or another!

Dick Shallow: We have all known a few of these SHALLOW, DICKs. Located in TX only, but there's more, we know it.

Dick Shame: This is what an overly-strict upbringing will do to a boy. Just one of these poor fellas was found, in AZ.

Dick Sharp: Careful! You'll poke somebody's eye out! Especially in AK, TX, OK, MO, IL, MT, IA, MI, OH, TN, FL, VA, MN, KS, CA, AZ, KY, and VA where these guys live.

Dick Shaver: Do I see a *five o'cock* shadow? He'll remove it using a **Dick Razor** and some **Dick Lather** (q.v.). Found in public phone books in Hale Center, TX; and Apex, NC. *See,* also: **Dick Head, Harry Dick,** and **Dick Face.**

*** CELEBRITY DICK ***

Dick Shawn: Actor, comedian (1923–1987). Played Adolf Hitler in Mel Brooks's *The Producers* (1968) and Ethel Merman's beatnik son Sylvester in Stanley Kubrick's *It's A Mad Mad Mad Mad World* (1963).

Dick Sheep: That's just…. wrong. One old guy in PA bears this name.

Dick Shift: If you don't have automatic transmission, this is what you've got. I guess. Remember the stories, back in the early 70s, before the Internet—when our knowledge of sex was based pretty much on what other ignorant people told us—about the woman whose boyfriend slipped "Spanish Fly" in her drink and she got so horny that after she wore out her boyfriend, she made it with the stick shift knob in his car? I think that story came from Dr. David Reuben's best seller, *Everything You Ever Wanted To Know About Sex But Were Afraid To Ask.* Boy, was that a book full of helpful—and accurate—information. Like about how some guys in Africa have little bells inserted under the skin of their dicks so they can make music during sex? Anyway, there's one Dick Shift in the whole country—listed as Richard—in CA.

Dick Shiner: We've all done that, in a manner of speaking. But this one proudly wears the name. He has an unlisted number in PA. *See,* also: **Dick Polisher.**

Dick Shiver: You know that brief whole-body shake you sometimes get involuntarily while you're using the urinal? That's the Dick Shiver. (George Carlin called it the "piss shiver"). The phone books only list them as Richard, but they are there, in ID, TX, TN, FL, GA, NC, TN and SC.

Dick Shore: You can always find him right next to **Dick Lake** and **Dick Beach** (q.v.). And in the public phone directories of Edisto Island, SC and Rock Hill, SC.

Dick Short: In the book it appears as SHORT, DICK: poor bastards…found in CA, TX, KS, MT, AL, TN.

Dick Show: Entertainment for women. And the name of a guy in New Jersey. And as Richard, they can be found all over the place: MI, SD, FL, OH, SC, PA, NJ, MT, MS, TX, UT, and ME.

Dick Shower: Kinky! But messy. If you're into it, look in AZ, FL, NY, PA, MS, WA (under Richard).

Dick Sick: A sick dick should be brought to a **Dick Doctor** (q.v.), or at the least a **Dick Nurse** (q.v.). As you can imagine, there are a lot of sick dicks out there (open wide and say ahhhhhh....). They are out there (as Richard) in NE, OH, FL, GA, NY and NC. Maybe you've met some of them.

Dick Siemens: Looking for him? Try the Chiloquin, OR phone book. *See,* also: **Dick Seamen.**

Dick Silk: One smooth character. Or four, if you're counting the public phone listings in La Vergne, TN; Murfreesboro, TN; and two different guys in Spokane, WA. *See,* also: **Silke Dick.**

Dick Singer: What a talent! Performing at a lounge near you in NC, PA, NH, ID, TX and FL.

Dick Sisters: I'm not going to stoop so low as to make a joke about this name. I'll let you do it. One poor SOB lives in DC with this moniker.

Dick Sizemore: A name that all men would like to earn. Perhaps he shops at the Big & Long stores. Just one in the phone books out there, in Tetonia, ID, and two Dicki Sizemores: one in Mount Juliet, TN and one San Antonio, TX.

Dick Slaughter: If it isn't a crime, it should be. "Dickslaughter: first degree." Not only are there several Dick Slaughters listed out there—in WA, AZ, TX, NC, and NV—but this book would not be complete if I did not mention **Dickiesue Slaughter,** who is listed as being in NV.

Dick Slave: Every man's fantasy girl. Not a great name for a man to have, I'd say. There appear to be three or four of them in the country (as Richard) with unlisted numbers in FL and CA. And of course, every Dick Slave needs a **Dick Master** (q.v.).

Dick Slayer: A guy who you call when you have trouble with **Dick Dragon** (*see* that listing). But you can only find him in LA.

Dick Slocum: What women look for after too many experiences with **Dick Quick, Dick Fast** and **Dick Trigger** (q.v.). Can also be a side-effect of certain anti-depressants such as Prozac and Paxil. Found only in the public phone books of Mears, MI and Mission, TX.

Dick Slow: When you've got the time, this is a nice way to do it. Just one out there (as Richard) in MA. If you're in a hurry, like during lunch time or if your husband is due home any minute, *see* **Dick Quick** or **Dick Fast.**

Dick Small: (Listed as SMALL, DICK) Hard to believe they would list themselves like this in public phone books, but there they are, in Auburn, ME and Newman Lake, WA.

Dick Smart: Sounds like a very large store where you go to buy your dicks. But it's just some guys in CA, OK, MI, and IN.

Dick Smelling: There's a Richard Smelling in WA, and that's close enough for me. Or anybody. *See also* **Dick Stank** and **Dick Sweater**.

Dick Smile: How do you make a dick smile? Tell him a joke. At least two guys by this name are in VT and NM.

Dick Smiley: Let a smiley dick be your umbrella. Found in Minneapolis, MN.

Dick Smiling: When you're dick's smiling, the whole world smiles with you. Isn't that how the song goes? One smiling Dick can be found (as Richard) in IA.

Dick Smoker: Bad enough to call a woman this name, it's cruel for a man. Unless he's a gay prostitute. Not surprisingly, this CA resident has an unlisted number.

Dick Smooth: How would you like to be a smooth dick? One guy (as Richard) in NC could tell you all about it.

*** CELEBRITY DICK ***

Dick Smothers (1937–) Half of the Smothers Brothers comedy team, which got cancelled by CBS for its biting anti-war and pro-integration satire in 1969.

Dick Snow: Awfully strange weather, to say the least. Found in Pocahontas, AR; Bellflower, CA; Adrian, MO; Efland, NC; Statesville, NC; Mount Vernon, OH; Echo, OR; Springville, UT and King, NC public phone books.

Dick Soldier: Can stand at attention for hours and fire on command. A good man to know, ladies. Found in the unlisted directories of ND, OK and WI (as Richard).

*** FICTIONAL DICK ***

Dick Solomon: Character played by John Lithgow (1945–) on TV sitcom *Third Rock From The Sun.*

Dick Sore: If you have a sore dick, hopefully it's just sore from enjoying yourself and not because you have a sore on your dick. The only SORE, DICKS out there call themselves Richard, but you can call them what you like…. at your own risk. There are at least two of them, in TN and NC.

Dick Soup: Probably a French recipe. They'll put anything in their mouths: snails, brains, Nazi dicks, truffles…. Do you know what a truffle is? It's a fungus that grows underground on the roots of oak trees. Do you know how the French find truffles? They hunt for them with a *pig*, whose highly-developed sense of smell makes them experts at finding these "delicacies." Who else but the French would eat a fungus that you need a pig to find? And then you even have to ask if they could really come up with a dick soup? One unlisted number record (as Richard) in CA. *See*, also: **Dick French.**

Dick Sparks: What you get when you press **Dick Steele** onto a **Dick Grinder** (q.v.). These Sparks fly in AL, WA, WV, NV, NM, and TX.

Dick Speaker: When stereo just isn't enough. One person in CA is listed.

Dick Speck: Somehow even worse than names like Dick Small and Dick Short, which are, after all, relative terms. But a "speck" is, by any definition, itsy-bitsy. A name like that could give a guy a complex. Could that have been what drove mass murderer **Richard Speck** to strangle eight student nurses back in 1966? Today, two men are found in public records with this name, in NM and TX.

Dick Spicer: Sounds like somebody who doesn't like their **Dick Bland** (q.v.). Just one of these gourmet-sounding names is found, in Cedar Park, TX.

Dick Spitt: One of the many idiomatic expressions for the fluids expelled from that wonderful appendage at the height of passion. As a name, however, it is not as popular; belonging, in fact, to just one citizen found in TX (as Richard).

Dick Spitter: You know, I almost feel bad listing a name like this, thinking about the poor guy who has to live with it…but am I the one who told him to go through life using the name Dick? He's listed only in Florida, but I'm thinking back to some ex-girlfriends.…

Dick Sprinkle: That is, after all, what they do, isn't it? So it makes sense. One gentleman in VA bears this name. *See,* also, **Dick Sprinkler.**

Dick Sprinkler: I'm not sure how efficient these would be in putting out a fire, and I'm sure the Building Department would not approve of such a system. Yet in FL and CO, two guys have made a name for it in the listings (as Ricky).

Dick Spitz: Well, they all do…at the appropriate moment, unless you have some kind of problem. These dudes are found (as Richard) in CA, TX, NE, IL, IN, OH, FL, NC, VA, PA, NY, SC, NV, CT, IA, WI, MD, NE, and ME.

Dick Sport: Is this a team sport like soccer, or a one-on-one like ping pong? Or maybe mixed doubles like tennis? I don't know, we're blazing a new trail. Make up your own rules. Dick Sport is played (under Richard) in PA, MA, AL, MO, and FL.

Dick Stank: No Dicks per se, but there is a Richard Stank in Arkansas, which, if you think about it, is close enough. We can call him Dick, hopefully from a good distance. Phew!

Dick Steele: If you're gonna build **Dick Bridges** or **Dick Towers** *(q.v.)*, you'll need plenty of Dick Steele. Where to find them? In Lake Havasu City, AZ; Laurel Hill, FL; Oelwein, IA; Piketon, OH; Grove, OK; Troutdale, VA; Oak Harbor, WA; Delta, CO; and Modesto, CA.

Dick Stiff: Stiff, Dick is shown as the name of at least three different guys with unlisted numbers in the AOL white pages.

Dick Stillwell: "How did your checkup go, Dear?" There's your answer, in AZ, MO, OH, CA, and FL.

Dick Stone: Geologists take note: These can be found in WA, OR, CA, ID, TX, AR, IL, MN, IA, OH, FL, NY, CO, WI, GA, NC, OK, TN, WI, and CA.

Dick Storm: It's coming down hard, but these don't usually last more than a few minutes. If you're one of those storm chasers, look for them (in the public phone books) of Arthur, IL; Topeka, KS; and Albemarle, NC.

Dick Story: Once upon a time, there were three little dicks.... And somebody blew, and blew, until.... To find out how it ends, look up Dick Story in Omaha, NE and Oklahoma City, OK.

Dick Strait: As it should be. *See,* also: **Dick Curley.**

Dick Strange: Listed as Strange, Dick, of course; four of these showed up in listings in CA, CO, VA and UT. Maybe you've had some.

Dick Strawberry: Another of the yummy flavors that Dick comes in. *See,* also, **Dick Chocolate, Dick Vanilla, Dick Cherry.** Found in RI and CA.

Dick Street: Okay, now here is a genuine, no-bullshit true fact: The Department of Corrections in Fayetteville, NC is located at 117 Dick Street. Also, an episode of the sitcom *Third Rock From The Sun* was entitled *Nightmare on Dick Street.* It originally aired on 18 May 1997. As for guys named Dick Street, there's one in Banner Elk, NC, and about five more in OR and TX. Too bad there's no Dick Street in Manhattan; it would make a great pair of signs at the intersection of Gay Street, in Greenwich Village, or at Seaman Avenue or Cumming Street, which are both located in the Inwood section of Manhattan and which, by the way, do intersect.

Dick Strong: Sounds like what Mongo say. Found in Mesa, AZ; Billings, MT; Grants Pass, OR; Salt Lake City, UT; Tulsa, OK; and Stevensville, VA.

Dick Stroker: To add to a name like this would just be gilding the lily. There's a guy in CA who is called…presumably proudly…by this name.

Dick Stubble: When you have this, it's time to visit **Dick Shaver** for a **Dick Shave** using a sharp **Dick Razor** and some hot **Dick Lather** (q.v.). Several guys by this name reside in MI, OH and IL.

Dick Stuff: Sounds like a men's erotic boutique, but it's just a guy with an unlisted number in IL.

Dick Stump: Result of a tragic circumcision accident? These poor souls can be found in CA, IN, NV, and MI.

Dick Succa: A most unfortunate name for a man to be saddled with, unless that's his stock in trade. At least two, and as many as four individuals known by this name are found in the unlisted number records, in CA and DC.

Dick Suck: There are two guys in Texas listed as Richard Suck. A sense of empathy forbids me from saying any more. You and your stupid friends can take it from here.

Dick Suckle: There are numerous listings in TX and CA for a number of different individuals named Richard Suckle.

Dick Sucker: Listed in the public phone book of Orlando, FL (and, while not a Dick, the Queens, NY phone book lists a "Cock Sucker" in Jackson Heights); people named Dick Sucker also have unlisted phone numbers in NY, NV, CO and IL.

Dick Sucky: What a lot of our soldiers got while stationed in Southeast Asia. And the name of a guy in Minnesota. Also found as Richard in MN, NY and PA.

Dick Sushi: Must be a hand roll. Amazingly, there is one in the records (as Riki) in CA.

Dick Sugar: What better way to sweeten your **Dick Coffee** (q.v.). This rare treat can be found with an unlisted number only in NY.

Dick Supreme: Leader of a tribe of sonofabitches? You know, the Supreme Dick? Or one of Diana Ross' old backup singers?

Dick Surprise: Like in "The Crying Game"? Three of them are found in AOL white pages with unlisted numbers.

Dick Swallow: A smaller branch of the Sucker family? Just one listed, in CA, but we KNOW there's more...!

Dick Sweat: Time for a shower, buddy! It's being worked up in OH, LA, GA, FL, NV, and TN.

Dick Sweater: This is what your mother makes you put on at the nude beach so it doesn't catch cold. To get yours, look in PA.

Dick Sweet: For some Sweet, Dick, look in Lansing, KS; Buffalo, NY; and Waldport, OR. Best part: it won't rot your teeth. (So is there a **Dick Bitter**? Thankfully, none were found, but *see* **Dick Sour**). In college, there was a guy in my dorm named Richard Sweet; giggling girls would call his room after seeing his name in the directory and ask him, "Are you *really* sweet?" To which he would always reply, "Why don't you eat me and find out?" He disappeared after our freshman year.

Dick Swelling: I recommend putting an ice pack on it. If you're looking for Dick Swelling, you can either try hitting it with a hard object or looking in VA, where he has an unlisted number.

Dick Swing: An Olympic event? Or something very kinky on the front porch? Considering where these names are found, I'd guess the latter: KY and TN.

Dick Switch: Wouldn't it be convenient if you could flick it "on" and "off" that easily? I'll bet women think so. So far there's just one dick switch out there (as Richard) in PA.

*** FICTIONAL DICK ***

Dick Swiveller: (1841) Literary character, from the novel *The Old Curiosity Shop* by Charles Dickens.

Dick Tack: Breath mint for gay guys? This one's only in CA.

Dick Tanner: Guys who don't like having tan lines, I guess. But they'd better use plenty of sunblock, or they might turn into **Dick Burns** (q.v.). Found in public phone books in Davis; CA; Colorado Springs, CO; Yoder, CO; Gulf Breeze, FL; Palm Beach, FL; Menlo, GA; Richardson, TX; and Dresser, WI.

Dick Tartar: A gourmet dish made from **Dick Raw** (q.v.). If you have a taste for it, look in TX, IN, CO, WA and IL (under Richard).

Dick Taster: Mmmmmm.... could use a dash more cilantro. There is one Dick Taster with an unlisted number in AZ, but you can probably find one in your local disco.

Dick Tate: The bossy type? Find them in TX, OK, MO and PA.

Dic Tater: Could it be a member of the Aryan Nations? Or just a guy with a sense of humor? Whatever he is, he's really out there. There's just one in the books, and that's how he spells his name. Located in SC.

Dick Taylor: Phallic fashion is their passion? Showrooms conveniently located in WA, OR, CA, NV, NM, AZ, UT, WY, TX, CO, OK, AR, LA, NE, MO, KS, IL, MT, MI, MN, IN, OH, KY, MS, AL, FL, NJ, ME and MA.

Dick Tax: They tax everything else; can this be far off? I found one person with this name, in NY.

Dick Tease: Wouldn't you love to know what having a name like this does to a guy's life? He's listed in the public phone book of New London, WI.

Dick Teller: Sounds like this prick can't keep a secret. Several listings in TX and ID.

Dick Temple: Oy, what a service! And the coffee and cake were excellent. Nu? They're in the phone book. In Saint James City, FL; Tarpon Springs, FL and Choctaw, OK.

*** WRESTLING DICK ***

Dick The Bruiser: (1929–1991) Professional wrestler and former NFL football player. 260 lbs of solid muscle, his neck was thicker than his head. Won 5 heavyweight wrestling titles from 1957–1962. Tough as nails, he was a ferocious brawler. Opponents used to go into the ring hoping to come out alive. Dropped dead of a heart attack after his usual morning workout in 1991.

Dick Thorn: Ouch!!! Send a tweezers to these guys in Chillicothe, IL; Sheridan, MT; and undisclosed addresses in OH and IA.

Dick Thunder: One of the greatest names in this book, and one of my personal favorites. Women get hot just hearing it (I would think). Found in the unlisted records for WA, CA, MI, WI, and WY (as Richard).

*** CELEBRITY DICK ***

Dick Tiddy: PGA Professional Golfer; One of Golf Magazine's Top 100 Teachers; played #3 behind Arnold Palmer and Buddy Worsham at Wake Forest.

*** FIGHTING DICK ***

Dick Tiger: (1929–1972) Boxing legend, inducted into the Hall of Fame. A native of Nigeria and a member of the Igbo tribe, he was a strong supporter of Biafran independence and spent a large part of his fortune supporting that losing struggle. Because he supported the rebels against the Nigerian government, he became an outcast. Tiger once said, "Our opponents call the Igbo the 'Jews of Africa.' It is meant as an insult. I interpret it as a high compliment." Frequently asked whether his people practiced cannibalism, he would respond, "We gave that up years ago when the Governor-General made us sick."

Dick Time: Isn't *any* time dick time? At least when you're single it is! There is just one public record out there, for a Richard, in CA.

Dick Tingle: I love when that happens! There's one listed in OH.

Dick Titman: Not one, but two of them (very appropriately) out there: NE and OR.

Dick Titter: Just one out there; he has a unlisted phone number in MD.

Dick Tock: The sound made by the clock in Michael Jackson's bedroom? When the big hand is on the dick, and the little hand is on the dick, it's **Dick Time** (q.v.). There are several Richard Tocks in this great land of ours, living in TX, IL, WI, OH, FL and MA.

Dick Tool: Another redundancy. One guy (listed as Richard) lives in NY.

Dick Tooth: A medical anomaly? Several listings in AOL white pages indicating unlisted numbers.

Dick Touch: Michael Jackson's other identity? Several different listings in AOL white pages, shown as unlisted. You would, too.

Dick Tower: Just one found.... in WA (near the Space Needle, perhaps?). *See,* also: **Dick Bridges, Dick Steele.**

Dick Toy: This one requires no additional joke. It is just...*there*, in all its glory. Six of them, in the public records. Not Richards, but Dicks (there are *dozens* of them listed as Richard). And they reside in NY, MA, IN and CA. To these gentlemen I just want to say...thank you for being there. We *all* thank you. Now go play with it.

*** LITERARY DICK ***

Dick Tracy: Comic Book detective invented by Chester Gould in 1931, whose gimmick was always using the latest in crime-fighting technology including the then-futuristic two-way wrist TV. In 1990, Warren Beatty directed and starred (along with Madonna and Al Pacino) in a truly third-rate and forgettable movie adaptation.

Dick Trainor: Now here's a guy we could all use, especially in our teens. because…I don't know about you, but mine didn't come with instructions, and I had to figure it out by trial and error. And I'll bet some wives out there would like to hire one for their hubbies. Fortunately there are several: NY, AR and CA.

Dick Trapp: Another name for a vagina? An underage hottie? Or an S&M device? These guys can be found in OH, TX, CA, and OR.

Dick Triangle: Oh, that's easy. You just take three dicks and…. you know. If they're all the same size you get an equilateral dick triangle. If they vary in size, you can make an isosceles dick triangle, or maybe even a right dick triangle if one of them is black. There's only one Dick Triangle in the listings (a Richard), in FL.

Dick Trick: Does it jump through hoops? Roll over? Play dead? Does it disappear and then he pulls it out of his ear? You'll have to go to Idaho to find out.

*** RACING DICK ***

Dick Trickle: Well-known NASCAR driver. His name sounds like a symptom of gonorrhea.

Dick Tricky: You have to go to Alaska to find this unique individual. *See,* also: **Dick Nixon.**

Dick Trigger: You don't want to be too fast on the dick trigger, or else your woman will be looking for **Dick Slocum** (q.v.). Leave your **Dick Gunn** in your **Dick Holster** (q.v.) for a good long time and she'll be a happy girl. The unlisted number records show this name (as Richard) in AL, MI, NY and TX.

Dick Trucks: Are these the ones advertised as "Ram Tough"? You can find them all over the **Dick Roads** (q.v.) and living in WI, AL, IA, and CA (as Richard).

Dick True: Because nobody likes false dick. Find your True Dick in IA, TX, and MA. *See also* **Dick Lyon**.

Dick Tuna: Comes in Solid White or Chunk Light. Either way…bad visual. At least two Dick Tunas are out there in the internet listings, in CA and NJ.

Dick Tung: Another medical condition. Symptoms: it's red, elongated and swollen, with a white discharge at the tip. One man with this name, if not the condition, resides in San Diego, CA, another in Florida.

Dick Turner: Didn't he play on *As The Dick Turns?* Anyway, there's a bunch of them out there: WA, OR, CA, NV, NM, UT, CO, TX, OK, AR, LA, MO, IL, MT, SD, WI, KY, TN, AL, FL, NC, VA, VT, and MA.

*** LEGENDARY DICK ***

Dick Turpin: (1706–1739) Robber, smuggler, housebreaker, highwayman, and horse thief in England. They finally hanged his ass in 1739. The passage of time has somehow made this scumbag a romantic figure.

Dick Tutcher: No Dicks found, but there's a Richard Tutcher in FL, and that's good enough for us, because let's face it…we are ALL Dick Tutchers.

Dick Uranus: With the kind of real names that are out there, I figured I'd search for this one. No, there is no Dick Uranus in the public records database. Not even a Richard. However, I did discover, to my surprise, that this is actually a family surname, with members in five states. Maybe someday they'll name a child Richard, and then a place will be earned in some future edition.

Dick Valet: If you don't want to be a **Dick Parker** (q.v.), do business with a place that has a Dick Valet. But they're pretty rare: found only in the internet public records listings of OR and IA.

*** CELEBRITY DICK ***

Dick Van Patten: Actor, star of 1980s sitcom *Eight Is Enough.*

*** CELEBRITY DICK ***

Dick Van Dyke: Actor best known for the 1960s sitcom *The Dick Van Dyke Show* and for his role opposite Julie Andrews in *Mary Poppins.* Also, his name sounds like a lesbian driving a truck full of dildoes.

Dick Vain: We've all known a few vain dicks in our time. Ok, it looks good, but not *that* good, I'm sure! Found in the unlisted books (as Richard) in MD, NJ, NY, FL and WI.

Dick Vane: When one of these guys is mounted on the roof of the farmhouse, he tells you which way the wind is blowing. Found in the unlisted directories of HI, TX, FL, MD, NY, IL, CA and WA (as Richard).

Dick Vein: Usually only seen in the company of **Dick Hard** (q.v.). Three of these gentleman grace the unlisted records (as Richard), in SC, MI and IL.

*** ATHLETIC DICK ***

Dick Vermeil: Football Coach, Head Coach Kansas City Chiefs Football team. One of only four head coaches to lead two different teams to the Super Bowl.

*** CELEBRITY DICK ***

Dick Vitale: (1939–) Sports Announcer for ESPN and ABC Sports.

Dick Wacker: Was he born with this name, or did he earn it? A real person, in NE.

Dick Wager: "I'll bet you $10 my dick's longer than yours!" "Ok, you're on!" Found in TN and MA, unlisted.

Dick Wagger: If you're looking for a Dick Wagger, you'll have to pay the fee to get the unlisted numbers of these guys: at least three, per the AOL white pages. Or just look in the mirror.

Dick Waggin: "Throw out your dicks! Throw out your dicks! The Dick Waggin is here!" No Dicks listed, but there's a Richard in PA…come on, that's a Dick Waggin!

Dick Warden: When you go to Dick Prison, he's the boss. CA, MT, WI, IA, OH, DE, DC, and CA.

Dick Warmer: A great thing to have when you go skiing or snow tubing. You can find them in CA, NH, DC, CA, MD and IL.

Dick Weed: Something that grows in dick gardens. I know they are more common than this; I've met plenty of them. This is a name with unlisted numbers in CA, IA, NV, OR, KY and PA. Always in conflict with **Dick Farmer** and **Dick Plant** (q.v.).

Dick Whitecock: The good news is that Whitecock does in fact exist as a family name. The bad new is: no Dicks or Richards, at least not in the public or unlisted phone records. *See,* also: **Dick Blackcock.**

*** CELEBRITY DICK ***

Dick Whittington (c 1350–1423) Legendary poor boy who became Lord Mayor of London. According to legend (translation: bullshit), Dick sends his cat on a merchant ship, to be sold. The ship arrives in Barbary, which is suffering a plague of mice and rats. The King of Barbary pays a huge sum of money for the cat, which the merchant brings back and gives to Dick, who spends the rest of his life as a wealthy merchant, Lord Mayor, etc. A fortune for a cat…. yeah, right. Someone once defined "legend" as "a lie which has attained the dignity of age."

Dick Wiener: Good name for a hot dog vendor. The AOL white pages say at least three guys have this lovely name.

Dick Withers: What a shame! Found in TX, MO, WV, and MS. Send Viagra!

Dick Wise: Hey, by the time your dick gets wise, it's too tired to do much. You can find wise dicks in ID, KS, IA, OH, KY, MO, TX, and FL.

*** CELEBRITY DICK ***

Dick Wolf: (1946–) Producer of TV dramas *Law and Order* and *Miami Vice.*

Dick Wood: What you get when you're excited; a product of the **Dick Forest** (q.v.) and/or, the guys who work with **Dick Carpenter** (q.v.). There's lots of Dick Woods around, including Luverne, AL; Mobile, AL; Rutledge, AL; Cardiff, CA; Mesa, AZ; Lemoore, CA; Naples, FL; Kokomo, IN; Kinston, NC; Sheridan, MT; Kitty Hawk, NC; South Sioux City, NE; Columbus, OH; Philo, OH; Broken Arrow, OK; Beech Island, SC; Georgetown, SC; Clinton, TN; Oak Ridge, TN; Bridgeport, TX; Bullard, TX; Longview, TX; Springtown, TX; Sugar Land, TX; Murray, UT; Oakley, UT; Arlington, VT; Chelan, WA; Kent, WA; Dallas, TX; Sonora, TX; Maryville, TN; Philadelphia, PA; Parkville, MD; Centerville, UT; South Deerfield, MA; and Longview, TX. And let's not forget **Dickson Wood** of Richmond, VA.

Dick Work: When the caveman's new bride was asked, "How's married life?" this was her happy answer. It's also the name of a guy in Tennessee.

Dick Worm: Hopefully it's not an inchworm. One guy with this name lives in MN. He might want to stay away from **Dick Fisher** (q.v.).

Dick Worth: Listed as WORTH, DICK, which is not exactly a compliment; find them in NE and FL.

Dick Worthy: Now, if you say this about a woman, it's a compliment! And it's also a guy living in GA.

Dick Worship: Must be what takes place in **Dick Church** and **Dick Temple** (q.v.), wouldn't you think? Several men are known by this name (as Richard), all in OH.

Dick Wurm: What were his parents thinking? This guy lives in OH with an unlisted number. And lord knows what else.

Dick Wyde: From what I'm told, it's *much* more important to be **Dick Wyde** than to be **Dick Long.** Three lucky men have this name (as Richard) in the unlisted records of WA and FL.

Dick Yanker: At least three guys with this name has unlisted numbers out there, according to AOL white pages, but haven't we all earned that title at one time or another?

*** CELEBRITY DICK ***

Dick York: (1928–1992) Actor. He was the first of two actors to play husband Darren opposite Elizabeth Montgomery on the 1960s sitcom *Bewitched.* The second Darren was **Dick Sargeant** (q.v.).

Dick Yuma: Sounds like prank phone call material. "Hello? Is Dick Yuma there? Yeah…Dick. Yuma. No…. YU—MA. DICK—YU—MA. Is he there? No?……" A real Dick Yuma is in the phone book in El Prado, NM.

Dick Yura. When you look in the telephone book and see a listing that reads Yura, Dick, you just have to sit back and wonder. OK, I have to be honest. The listings all read Richard. But so what? If your surname is Yura, and you get named Richard, then you cannot hide from the forces which dictate that Richards are called Dick, and ipso facto, Yura Dick. There are several of these gentlemen, in NJ, PA and VA.

Dick Youseff: A suggestion often made in anger. And one man in OH has to hear it every day (as Richard). Also: **Dick Yusef,** in CA.

Dick Zappa: Frank's lesser-known and less-successful sibling. Made the bottom of the freak-rock charts with cheap attempts to rip off Frank's songs, like

Snow: If It's Yellow, I Wouldn't Eat It; Overcooked Weenie Sandwich; Transformer Humm; Soiled Napkins; and *Don't Take My Picture While I'm Sitting On The Toilet.* Today, Dick lives in MN with an unlisted telephone number, with his children Hamed, Diesel, Pluto and Sheeba.

Dick Zero: I think I would go to court before I would be listed anywhere as Zero, Dick. But two guys listed in DC and NJ don't seem to mind. Who knows, maybe it's an accurate description.

Dick Zip: Not as bad as Zero, Dick, but who wants to be listed alphabetically anywhere as "Zip, Dick"? AZ and MI are home to two persons named Richard Zip, both of whom are unlisted.

Postscript

Now, remember, dumb-asses, DON'T call any of the people mentioned in this book, or make any attempt to contact them. Just because we had a few stupid laughs together doesn't mean you have a license to go make yourself a pain in the ass to innocent people.

And DON'T go doing something stupid and later tell some judge that THIS BOOK influenced you to do it. You are NOT...I repeat: NOT...to break any law, to contact anyone (by internet, telephone, mail, or otherwise), to annoy or harass anyone, or to otherwise behave like an untrained chimpanzee who has been released from his cage by PETA activists, and then have the *nerve*—on your own or on the advice of some greasy lawyer that your parents hire for you—to blame ME or anybody else for the fact that YOU were not raised correctly or that you are genetically damaged by all the drugs and/or alcohol that you and/or your parents have ingested.

I hope you enjoyed this book, and will continue to enjoy it for a long time to come. Have fun, and remember, above all: DON'T BE A DICK! But if you *must* be a dick, be a good one!

Larry Rogak
Oceanside, New York
March 2005

About the Author

This is Larry Rogak's second comedy book. He is an attorney in New York who practices "insurance defense," which means that when some idiot uses her crotch as a cup holder for boiling hot coffee and gets burned, he tries to stop her from making money for her own stupidity.

Originally from Brooklyn, Larry grew up on a tough block but was not tough himself. He learned by instinct that by making other kids laugh, he could sometimes avoid getting his ass kicked. Darwin would call this adaptive behavior. The ability to run pretty fast also helped.

Larry attended the University of Miami, Florida, from 1974–1978 where he became proficient in pinball at the Student Union. This was the pre-video game era, although by 1978, "Pong" had appeared in table-top versions at trendy bars. Graduating with a B.A. in Philosophy, Larry had little choice but to go to law school. He came back to Brooklyn to do so.

Today Larry lives with his wife, their four children, three dogs, and dozens of ducks, on Long Island.

If you didn't like *You Don't Know Dick,* then you'll probably hate his first comedy book, *Haiku For Guys*.

978-0-595-35433-7
0-595-35433-5

Printed in the United States
29070LVS00007B/11

9 780595 354337